The Technique of Embellishments: Crafting with Buttons, Sequins, Beads, and More

Andrew Darren Steele

Published by Steele Andrew Darren, 2024.

THE TECHNIQUE OF EMBELLISHMENTS: CRAFTING WITH BUTTONS, SEQUINS, BEADS, AND MORE

First edition. March 31, 2024.

Copyright © 2024 Andrew Darren Steele.

ISBN: 979-8224474141

Written by Andrew Darren Steele.

Table of Contents

Chapter 1: Buttons

- Introduction to Buttons

Dive into the world of DIY embellishments! In this comprehensive guide, we will delve into the fascinating realm of buttons, starting with an introduction that will set the stage for your creative journey. Buckle up as we explore the many possibilities and techniques with buttons!.

Buttons, with their vast array of shapes, sizes, and materials, are a versatile and indispensable component in the world of crafting. They can add a touch of elegance, whimsy, or even a vintage appeal to any project. Whether you are a beginner or an experienced artisan, buttons offer endless opportunities to express your creativity.

The world of buttons is expansive and diverse, and it is crucial to familiarize ourselves with the different types of buttons available. Buttons can be crafted from a variety of materials, including paper, beads, sequins, rhinestones, gemstones, charms, pom-poms, feathers, felt, cork, washi tape, fabric tape, duct tape, masking tape, glitter, glitter glue, sequin waste, tinsel, foil, and aluminum foil. Each material offers its unique texture, color, and visual appeal, making it suitable for specific projects or themes.

Sequins, for example, are ideal for adding a sparkle and shine to garments, accessories, or even home decor items. Their reflective surface catches the light and instantly adds glamour to any project. Similarly, beads come in various sizes, shapes, and colors, making them perfect for intricate beadwork or adding subtle embellishments.

Rhinestones and gemstones are prized for their luxurious and captivating appearance. Perfect for formal attire, jewelry making, or adding a touch of opulence to any creation. Charms, on the other hand, exude a whimsical and playful vibe, often used in jewelry making or scrapbooking.

For those looking to add texture and dimension to their projects, pom-poms, feathers, and felt are excellent choices. The softness of feathers, the fluffiness of pom-poms, and the versatility of felt bring a tactile element that instantly elevates any craft. And for those who seek unconventional materials, cork, washi tape, fabric tape, duct tape, masking tape, glitter, glitter glue, sequin waste, tinsel, foil, and aluminum foil offer exciting possibilities to explore.

As you venture into the world of button crafting, it is essential to consider the nature of your project, the theme you wish to convey, and the desired aesthetic. Selecting the right button material will ensure a harmonious and visually appealing final result.

Now that you have been introduced to the intriguing world of buttons, it's time to roll up your sleeves and embark on your DIY journey. Experiment, explore, and unleash your imagination to create one-of-a-kind masterpieces that reflect your unique style and creativity.

Remember, the possibilities are endless, and with the right buttons, your creations will dazzle and delight. So, gather your materials, let your creativity soar, and enjoy the rewarding experience of crafting with buttons! Happy embellishing!.

- Different Types of Buttons

Buttons are a versatile and stylish addition to any DIY project. They come in a wide variety of materials and designs, allowing you to achieve the perfect look for your creations. From paper crafts to rhinestones, charms, and feathers, the possibilities are endless!.

Paper Crafts for Buttons.

One unique and creative way to make buttons is by using paper crafts. You can easily create your own paper buttons by using various techniques. One option is to simply cut out small circles or shapes from colorful or patterned paper. Then, using a button-making kit or a button machine, attach a plastic or metal button back to your paper cutouts. This will create a custom and personalized button that you can use for embellishments on clothing, accessories, or home decor items.

Sequins.

Sequins are a widely used embellishment material and can also be used to create unique buttons. To make sequin buttons, you will need a button mold or base, sequins, and adhesive. Start by applying a small amount of adhesive to the button mold or base. Then, carefully place the sequins on top of the adhesive, arranging them in a desired pattern or design. Allow the adhesive to dry completely before using your sequin buttons.

Beads.

Beads are another popular choice for creating buttons. They come in a variety of shapes, sizes, and colors, allowing you to create buttons that suit your project perfectly. To make bead buttons, you will need a button mold or base, beads, and adhesive. Begin by applying a thin layer of adhesive to the button mold or base. Then, place the beads onto the adhesive, creating a pattern or design. You can mix and match different bead types to add texture and visual interest to your buttons.

Rhinestones.

If you're looking to add some sparkle and glam to your projects, rhinestone buttons are an excellent choice. To make rhinestone buttons, you will need a button mold or base, rhinestones, and adhesive. Similar to the process of making sequin buttons, apply adhesive to the button mold or base and carefully place the rhinestones on top. You can create intricate designs or opt for a more minimalist look by using a single rhinestone in the center of the button.

Gemstones.

For a more elegant and luxurious touch, consider using gemstones to create buttons. Gemstone buttons can instantly elevate the look of any project, adding a touch of sophistication. To make gemstone buttons, you will need a button mold or base, gemstones, and adhesive. Apply adhesive to the button mold or base and place the gemstones on top. You can choose to use a single gemstone or create a mosaic pattern using multiple gemstones.

Charms.

Charms are small, decorative items that can be easily turned into buttons. They come in a wide variety of designs, such as flowers, animals, or abstract shapes. To create charm buttons, you will need a button mold or base, charms, and adhesive. Apply adhesive to the button mold or base and carefully place the charm on top. Charms are a great way to add a personalized touch to your projects, making them extra special.

Pom-poms, feathers, felt, cork, washi tape, fabric tape, duct tape, masking tape, glitter, glitter glue, sequin waste, tinsel, foil, and aluminum foil are some other materials that can be used to make unique and eye-catching buttons. Each material has its own unique properties and can add a different texture or visual element to your buttons.

With this comprehensive guide on DIY buttons, you can now explore a wide range of materials and techniques to create your own unique and personalized buttons. Get creative, experiment with different materials, and let your imagination run wild. The possibilities are endless, and your buttons will surely make a statement in your craft projects!.

- Button Crafts Ideas

Buttons are versatile and can be easily transformed into beautiful crafts that add flair and style to any project. Whether you are a seasoned crafter or just starting out, this guide will provide you with a plethora of ideas and inspiration.

Let's begin with DIY Paper Crafts for Buttons. Paper crafts are an excellent way to showcase the beauty of buttons while creating unique and intricate designs. One idea is to create a button flower bouquet using colorful buttons of different sizes and shapes. Start by drawing or printing a flower template on cardstock paper, then cut out the flower shape. Next, arrange your buttons on the paper flower, gluing them in place. Add details such as button centers and stems with green paper or thread. This craft can be framed or used as a handmade greeting card.

Sequins are another fantastic embellishment that can be combined with buttons to create stunning crafts. One idea is to make a sequin and button unicorn. Start by drawing or printing a unicorn template on cardstock paper. Cut it out and use craft glue to attach colorful sequins on the unicorn's body, creating a beautiful sparkling effect. Use buttons for its eyes and nose, and add a button horn on its forehead. This craft can be used as a wall decoration or a fun addition to a child's room.

Beads are an excellent addition to any button craft project, as they provide texture and shine. One idea is to create a beaded button bracelet. Start by choosing a selection of buttons and beads that complement each other in color and style. Thread a needle with elastic cord or stretchy beading thread. String the buttons and beads onto the cord, creating an attractive pattern. Knot the ends of the cord together to close the bracelet. This accessory will add a pop of color and individuality to any outfit.

Rhinestones and gemstones can elevate the glamour of button crafts. One idea is to make a rhinestone button brooch. Start by selecting a large, flat button as the base of the brooch. Use a strong adhesive to attach rhinestones around the edges of the button, creating a dazzling border. Add a gemstone in the center for an extra touch of elegance. Attach a pin backing to the button using strong glue or a hot glue gun. This brooch can be worn on clothing or added to a scarf or bag for a touch of sparkle.

Charms can be a playful addition to button crafts, adding a touch of personality. One idea is to create a charm necklace using buttons and small metal charms. Start by selecting a chain necklace and attaching a jump ring to the end. Thread buttons and charms onto the jump ring, alternating between different designs and sizes. Repeat this process until the necklace reaches the desired length. This accessory will be a unique and eye-catching addition to any outfit.

Pom-poms, feathers, and felt are materials that can be used alongside buttons to create tactile and whimsical crafts. One idea is to make a button and pom-pom bookmark. Start by cutting a piece of felt into a rectangular shape. Glue a pom-pom to one corner of the felt, then attach buttons of various sizes and colors along the opposite edge. Add a feather to the top corner for an extra touch of fun. Use this bookmark to mark your place in your favorite books.

Cork, Washi tape, fabric tape, duct tape, masking tape, glitter, glitter glue, sequin waste, tinsel, foil, and aluminum foil are additional materials that can be incorporated into button crafts to add texture, color, and shine. Get creative and experiment with these materials, allowing your imagination to guide you.

Remember, the possibilities are endless when it comes to crafting with buttons, so have fun and enjoy the process of creating unique and personalized pieces. Happy crafting!.

Chapter 2: Sequins

- Introduction to Sequins

Sequins are fantastic embellishments that can add glamour, sparkle, and texture to any DIY project. In this chapter, we will explore the different types of sequins available, their various uses, and some creative techniques to incorporate sequins into your crafts.

Sequins come in a wide range of shapes, sizes, and materials. The most common shapes include round, square, teardrop, and star, but you can also find sequins in more intricate shapes like flowers, hearts, and animals. When it comes to size, sequins can vary from tiny micro-sequins, which are great for delicate details, to large statement sequins that instantly catch the eye.

One of the first decisions you'll need to make when working with sequins is choosing the right material. Depending on your project and personal preference, you can opt for sequins made of plastic, metal, fabric, or even natural materials like wood or shell. Each material has its own unique qualities and characteristics, so it's worth experimenting with different types to discover your favorite.

To attach sequins to your DIY projects, you have several options. The most common method is sewing them on using a needle and thread. This technique works well for fabrics, garments, and accessories. If sewing is not your preferred method, you can also use fabric glue or hot glue to secure the sequins in place. It's important to test the adhesive on a small scrap of fabric or material before applying it to your project to ensure it adheres properly.

Sequins can be used in a variety of crafts, including but not limited to clothing, accessories, home decor, and paper crafts. On the subject of paper crafts, button sequins can be an excellent choice. Button sequins, as the name suggests, are sequins shaped like buttons. They have two holes instead of the traditional single hole and can be easily sewn onto paper or cardstock using a needle and thread. This technique allows you to create stunning and intricate designs on greeting cards, scrapbook pages, and art journals.

Another approach to incorporating sequins into paper crafts is by using adhesive sheets or tapes. These sheets are pre-backed with a strong adhesive, making it simple to attach sequins without the need for sewing or glue. Simply peel off the backing, position the sequins on your project, and press them down firmly. You can create beautiful borders, patterns, or even entire backgrounds using this method.

When working with sequins, consider experimenting with different colors, textures, and sizes to create visual interest and dimension. Mixing and matching sequins of varying sizes and shapes can add depth and complexity to your projects. Additionally, incorporating sequins of different finishes, such as matte, metallic, or iridescent, can further enhance the overall aesthetic.

Whether you're adding a touch of sparkle to a clothing item, creating a decorative element for your home, or embellishing paper crafts, sequins can be a fantastic addition. With the right materials and techniques, you can unlock endless possibilities for creativity and self-expression.

- Types of Sequins

Sequins are one of the most versatile and popular embellishments used in DIY crafts. They add sparkle, glamour, and texture to any project, making them a favorite choice among artisans.

One type of sequin commonly used in DIY crafts is the classic flat sequin. These sequins are made of a shiny material, usually plastic or metallic, and come in various shapes and sizes. They can be round, square, rectangular, or even custom-shaped, allowing you to unleash your creativity and experiment with different designs. Flat sequins are ideal for adding a touch of glitz to clothing, accessories, and home decor items.

Another popular option is cup sequins. As the name suggests, these sequins have a small cup shape, which creates depth and dimension. Cup sequins are often used in embroidery and sewing projects, as they can be easily attached with a needle and thread. Due to their concave shape, they reflect light in a unique way, resulting in a stunning visual effect.

For those who want to add a touch of luxury to their crafts, sequins with seed beads are the perfect choice. These sequins are embellished with tiny beads, creating a mesmerizing texture and intricate detailing. The combination of sequins and beads adds depth and richness to any project, making it visually captivating.

If you're looking for sequins with a bit of flair, holographic sequins are an excellent option. These sequins have a holographic or iridescent finish, which gives them a mesmerizing color-changing effect when viewed from different angles. Holographic sequins are widely used in fashion and accessory design, as they instantly grab attention and make a bold statement.

Sequins are not limited to traditional shapes and sizes. You can find sequins in unique and whimsical designs, such as stars, hearts, flowers, animals, and more. These specialty sequins allow you to add a personalized and playful touch to your crafts, making them perfect for children's projects, festive decorations, and themed events.

Sequins are available in a vast array of colors, ranging from vibrant and bold to soft and pastel. This wide color palette gives you endless possibilities to incorporate sequins into your crafts and create different moods and looks. Whether you're aiming for elegance, glamour, or a pop of color, you'll find sequins in the shade that perfectly complements your artistic vision.

To incorporate sequins into your DIY projects, you will need a few basic supplies. These include a craft glue or adhesive, preferably one that dries clear and is suitable for fabric or paper, depending on your chosen base material. Additionally, a pair of tweezers or a small craft pick can be helpful for precise placement of sequins, especially for intricate designs.

Sequins can be attached individually or in patterns, allowing you to unleash your creativity and experiment with different techniques. You can sew them onto fabric, glue them onto paper or other surfaces, or even thread them onto thin wires for hanging decorations or jewelry making. The possibilities are endless, and the choice of attachment method depends on the overall look and feel you want to achieve.

Remember to have fun and experiment as you incorporate sequins into your DIY projects. Play with different shapes, sizes, colors, and textures to create unique and eye-catching embellishments. Let your imagination soar and transform ordinary crafts into extraordinary masterpieces with the help of sequins.

- Sequin Crafts Ideas

Sequins have long been a popular choice when it comes to crafting and embellishing various DIY projects. With their shimmering and reflective properties, they can add a touch of elegance and glamour to any creation.

When it comes to DIY paper crafts, sequins can be used in a myriad of creative ways. One popular idea is to use sequins to create stunning and eye-catching greeting cards. Simply adhere sequins to the front of your card using craft glue, and let your imagination run wild. You can arrange them in specific patterns or create beautiful designs, such as flowers, hearts, or even a twinkling night sky. The possibilities are endless!.

Sequins can also be incorporated into paper crafts for buttons. Create your own unique buttons by covering them with sequins. Start by finding a button mold or base, then glue sequins onto the front surface, ensuring they are evenly spaced and fully adhered. Once dry, you can attach these dazzling sequined buttons to clothing, bags, or any other fabric item you desire.

You can also use sequins to add a touch of sparkle to jewelry and accessories. For example, create a glamorous sequin necklace by stringing sequins onto beading wire, alternating them with other beads or gemstones for a dynamic and eye-catching design. Finish off with a clasp, and you'll have a stunning piece of jewelry that can dress up any outfit.

In addition to jewelry, sequins can also be used to embellish clothing. Whether you're adding them to a plain T-shirt, a pair of jeans, or even a scarf, sequins can instantly transform an ordinary item into a fashion statement. Use fabric glue or a needle and thread to attach sequins securely to the desired garment, and let your creativity shine.

From home decor to party decorations, there are countless ways to incorporate sequins into your creations. Create a sparkling sequined wall art piece by arranging sequins in a specific pattern or design on a canvas or wooden board. Alternatively, make your own sequined party banners or table centerpieces for special occasions.

Remember, the key to creating stunning sequin crafts lies in careful planning, attention to detail, and precision. Take the time to envision your final design and experiment with different arrangements and combinations. Whether you're adding a few sequins for a subtle touch or going all out with a dazzling display, sequins are sure to add a touch of magic to your DIY projects. So let your creativity run wild and enjoy the mesmerizing beauty of sequin crafts!.

Chapter 3: Beads

- Introduction to Beads

Beads are one of the most versatile and popular embellishments used in DIY crafts. They come in various shapes, sizes, and materials, offering endless possibilities for creativity and personalization. In this chapter, we will delve into the wonderful world of beads and explore different types of beads that you can incorporate into your DIY projects.

Buttons are a type of bead that you may already be familiar with. However, they deserve a special mention in this guide as they can be used not only as functional closures but also as decorative elements. Buttons come in a wide range of colors, styles, and materials, allowing you to choose the perfect ones for your project. Whether you want to add a vintage touch with antique buttons or create a quirky design with novelty buttons, buttons are a versatile bead that can enhance any DIY craft.

Sequins are another type of bead that adds sparkle and shine to any project. These small, flat discs can be sewn onto fabric or glued onto various surfaces. They come in different shapes, such as round, square, and heart, and are available in a multitude of colors. Sequins can instantly transform a plain item into a glamorous piece, making them a favorite among DIY enthusiasts.

Moving on to beads, which are perhaps the most popular type of embellishment. Beads are small decorative objects with a hole through which they can be threaded. They are commonly used in jewelry making but can also be incorporated into other crafts like textiles, home decor, and accessories. Beads are available in an extensive range of materials, such as glass, wood, ceramic, metal, plastic, and gemstones, allowing you to select the perfect beads for your project based on the desired aesthetic and theme.

Rhinestones are a type of gemstone bead that are often used to add a touch of glamour and elegance to DIY projects. These shimmering stones come in various sizes, shapes, and colors, and can be glued onto fabric or metal surfaces. Rhinestones are popularly used in jewelry making, dance costumes, and even interior decor items.

Gemstones, as the name suggests, are naturally occurring minerals that are cut and polished for use in various crafts. They are often used in jewelry making, as their unique colors and patterns add a touch of luxury and sophistication. Gemstone beads can be incorporated into DIY projects like bracelets, necklaces, and earrings, giving them a distinctive and high-end look.

Charms are small decorative pendants that add a personal touch to DIY crafts. These beads are often made of metal or plastic and are available in a wide range of designs and motifs. Charms can be attached to jewelry, keychains, and even bookmarks, allowing you to express your individuality and style.

Pom-poms are fluffy, ball-shaped beads made of yarn or fabric. They are commonly used in children's crafts, accessories like hats and scarves, and even home decor items. Pom-poms add a playful and whimsical touch to any DIY project, making them a favorite among crafters of all ages.

Feathers are unique and eye-catching bead options that bring a natural and ethereal element to your crafts. They can be used in various ways, such as earrings, headbands, or even as accents on larger items like dreamcatchers or costume accessories. Feathers allow you to create a boho-inspired or a strikingly elegant look, depending on their size and colors.

Felt is a versatile material that can be transformed into different shapes and forms, including beads. Felt beads are lightweight, soft, and can be easily sewn or glued onto various surfaces. They add a tactile and cozy feel to your DIY projects, making them ideal for items like jewelry, brooches, and home decor accents.

Cork is another unique material that can be used to create beads. Cork beads are lightweight, eco-friendly, and have a natural texture that adds an organic and earthy touch to your crafts. They can be painted or left in their natural state, making them ideal for jewelry, home decor, and even fashion accessories.

Washi tape, fabric tape, duct tape, and masking tape are not traditional beads, but they can be used to create beads-like elements in your projects. These adhesive tapes come in various colors, patterns, and textures, allowing you to easily create beads by rolling them up or cutting them into desired shapes. These tape beads can be incorporated into jewelry, accessories, and even home decor items.

Lastly, we come to glitter, glitter glue, sequin waste, tinsel, foil, and aluminum foil. While not typical forms of beads, these materials can be used to create bead-like elements in your DIY projects. Glitter, glitter glue, and sequin waste can be sprinkled or glued onto paper, fabric, or other surfaces to create shimmering bead effects. Tinsel, foil, and aluminum foil can be twisted or shaped into bead forms and used in various crafts. These materials add sparkle, texture, and dimension to your projects, allowing you to achieve unique and eye-catching results.

From buttons to gemstones, each type of bead offers its own distinct characteristics, allowing you to express your creativity and style. Incorporating beads into your projects can elevate them to new heights, adding visual interest, texture, and personality. So unleash your imagination, experiment with different types of beads, and let your DIY creations shine with their exquisite embellishments.

- Different Types of Beads

Beads are a versatile craft material that can add a touch of elegance and creativity to any project. Whether you are a seasoned artisan or just starting out in the realm of DIY, this guide will provide you with all the necessary information and inspiration to create dazzling beadwork.

Beads come in various shapes, sizes, and materials, each offering its own unique artistic potential. From classic glass beads to rustic wooden beads and everything in between, there is no shortage of options when it comes to bead selection. The type of bead you choose will largely depend on the desired aesthetic and purpose of your project.

Glass beads are a popular choice for their clarity and brilliance. They come in an array of colors, shapes, and finishes, such as iridescent, matte, or metallic. Glass beads are versatile and can be used in a multitude of crafts, including jewelry making, embroidery, and home décor.

For a more earthy and organic look, consider incorporating wooden beads into your DIY projects. These beads are available in various natural tones and grains, allowing you to create pieces with a rustic charm. Wooden beads are perfect for creating bohemian-style jewelry, macrame wall hangings, or even adding a touch of nature to your home décor.

Metal beads, on the other hand, can add a sleek and sophisticated element to your crafts. Whether it's sterling silver, gold-plated, or copper beads, they lend a luxurious touch to any project. Metal beads work well in jewelry making, embellishing clothing, or adding a shiny accent to handmade accessories.

If you are looking to add a bit of sparkle and glamour, consider using crystal or rhinestone beads. These beads are crafted from faceted glass or acrylic and are known for their dazzle and shine. They can be used to create exquisite jewelry pieces, embellish clothing or accessories, or add a touch of elegance to home decor.

Gemstone beads offer a touch of natural beauty and are considered more precious than other types of beads. With an extensive variety of gemstones available, including amethyst, turquoise, and jade, you can create stunning jewelry pieces that reflect the natural world. Each gemstone has its own unique healing properties and symbolism, making them not only visually appealing but also meaningful.

Charms are a delightful addition to any bead project, allowing you to personalize your creations. Charms come in various shapes and designs, such as animals, letters, or symbols, and can be easily incorporated into bracelets, necklaces, or keychains. They make wonderful gifts and can showcase the recipient's personality and interests.

Pom-poms, feathers, and felt beads introduce a playful and whimsical element to your DIY projects. These soft and tactile materials can be used to create fun accessories, such as earrings, hair clips, or even quirky home decor items. Pom-poms add a pop of color and texture, while feathers bring a touch of bohemian elegance. Felt beads, with their soft and cozy feel, are perfect for creating plush toys or embellishing clothing and accessories.

Moving away from traditional materials, you can also explore unconventional options for bead creation. Cork beads, which are made from agglomerated cork, are lightweight and eco-friendly. They can be painted, embellished, or left in their natural state to add an interesting texture to your projects.

Washi tape, fabric tape, duct tape, and masking tape beads offer a unique twist on conventional bead-making by utilizing sticky tapes. These tapes are layered and twisted to create beads that can be used in various crafts, such as jewelry, home decor, or scrapbooking. The versatility of tapes allows you to experiment with different colors and patterns, adding a contemporary and bold look to your creations.

For a touch of shimmer and shine, sparkle up your beadwork with glitter beads. These beads are coated with fine glitter, adding a touch of sparkle and glamour to your projects. Glitter beads are perfect for jewelry making, personalized accessories, or adding an eye-catching element to your home decor.

If you prefer a more subtle approach, glitter glue can be used to add a hint of sparkle to your bead creations. Simply apply the glue to your chosen beads and let it dry to achieve a subtle yet enchanting touch. Glitter glue is a versatile tool that can be used on various bead types, allowing you to customize the level of sparkle to suit your preferences.

Sequin waste, tinsel, foil, and aluminum foil beads offer unconventional and eye-catching alternatives. Sequin waste refers to the discarded film left behind after sequins are punched out, and it can be used to create unique and mesmerizing beads. Tinsel beads, crafted from strands of metallic or colored plastic, add a festive and playful touch to your creations. Foil beads can be made by wrapping strips of foil around a core, resulting in shiny and textured beads. Similarly, aluminum foil beads are made using aluminum foil, creating lightweight and malleable beads that can be manipulated into various shapes and designs.

Whether you prefer classic glass beads, natural gemstones, or unconventional materials such as sequin waste or aluminum foil, there is a bead type that will suit your artistic vision. By exploring the different options available and experimenting with various techniques, you can create truly unique and captivating beadwork that will elevate your DIY projects to new heights.

- Bead Crafts Ideas

Beads are versatile craft supplies that can add a touch of elegance and creativity to various projects. From jewelry making to home decor, bead crafts offer endless possibilities.

Let your imagination run wild as you choose from an array of beads such as glass beads, plastic beads, wooden beads, seed beads, and more. Experiment with various sizes, shapes, and colors to create unique pieces that reflect your personal style.

1. Jewelry Making:

Beaded jewelry is a popular craft that allows you to create beautiful and customized accessories. You can make bracelets, necklaces, earrings, or even anklets using different types of beads. Combine beads of various textures and colors to create eye-catching designs. The process involves stringing beads onto a wire, thread, or elastic cord, and securing them with clasps or knots.

2. Beaded Home Decor:

Add a touch of elegance to your home by incorporating beads into your decor. Create beaded curtains, lampshades, or even beaded fringe for pillows or curtains. Beaded coasters, placemats, or table centerpieces can enhance your dining experience. Use beads to embellish picture frames, vases, or candle holders, turning ordinary objects into stunning works of art.

3. Hair Accessories:

Beaded hair accessories are a great way to add a pop of color to your hairstyle. Create beaded hairpins, headbands, or barrettes to match your outfits or special occasions. You can also use beads to embellish plain hair ties or create unique hair jewelry.

4. Beaded Embroidery:

Beaded embroidery is a fascinating art form that combines beads and needlework. You can add beads to fabric, canvas, or even paper to create intricate and tactile designs. Beaded embroidery can be used to decorate clothing, accessories, or even wall art. Experiment with different stitches, bead sizes, and colors to add depth and texture to your embroidery projects.

5. Beaded Keychains:

Personalize your keys or give them as gifts by creating beaded keychains. Choose beads that reflect your interests, such as animal-shaped beads, letter beads, or beads in your favorite colors. Combine beads with charms or tassels to add extra flair. Beaded keychains are not only practical but also a fun way to express your creativity.

6. Beaded Accessories:

Take your accessory game to the next level by adding beads to hats, bags, or even shoes. Create beaded patches or use beads to accentuate existing patterns or designs. Beads can instantly transform everyday accessories into fashion-forward statement pieces.

Remember to let your creativity shine and experiment with different bead shapes, sizes, and materials. Play with color combinations and explore various techniques such as stringing, weaving, or embroidery. The possibilities are endless when it comes to DIY bead crafts. Enjoy the process and let your unique bead creations be a true reflection of your style and individuality.

Chapter 4: Rhinestones

- Introduction to Rhinestones

Rhinestones, dazzling and shimmering, can add a touch of glamour and sophistication to any DIY project. Whether you're embellishing a garment, jewelry, or home decor item, rhinestones are a wonderful addition. In this chapter, we will delve into the world of rhinestones and explore various ways to incorporate them into your crafts. From learning about different types of rhinestones to understanding the techniques involved, this guide will equip you with the knowledge you need to create stunning DIY projects with rhinestones.

To begin, let's grasp the basics of rhinestones. Rhinestones are decorative crystal or glass stones, resembling diamonds, that are used to adorn various items. They come in different shapes, sizes, colors, and finishes, allowing you to choose the perfect rhinestone for your project. From classic clear rhinestones that exude elegance to vibrant colored rhinestones that add a pop of personality, the options are truly endless.

When working with rhinestones, it's essential to gather the necessary tools and materials. Apart from the rhinestones themselves, you will need adhesive or glue, a toothpick or tweezers for precise placement, and a clean surface to work on. Depending on the nature of your project, you may also require additional supplies such as fabric, jewelry findings, or a hot-fix applicator.

One important consideration when using rhinestones is the adhesive or glue you choose. Different adhesives work best with specific materials, so it's crucial to select the right one for your project. Be sure to read the instructions provided by the manufacturer to ensure proper application. Test a small area first to ensure that the adhesive is compatible with your chosen surface.

Before adhering the rhinestones, it is advisable to plan your design. Mark the desired placement of the rhinestones on your project, creating a rough sketch or using a template if necessary. This helps maintain symmetry and visual appeal. Depending on the nature of your project, you may choose to create a pattern or follow a more random arrangement. The choice is entirely up to you and should align with your overall design vision.

Once you have planned your design, it's time to start applying the rhinestones. There are various techniques that can be employed based on the type of rhinestones you have chosen. If you're working with rhinestones that have a flat back, you can use glue or adhesive to affix them securely. Ensure that you apply the adhesive sparingly and precisely to avoid any overflow or messiness.

On the other hand, if you have opted for hot-fix rhinestones, a hot-fix applicator is required. These rhinestones are designed with a heat-sensitive adhesive on the back, allowing them to be securely attached using heat. Simply place the rhinestone in the desired location, apply heat with the hot-fix applicator, and carefully press down to ensure proper adhesion. This method is particularly useful when working with fabrics or textiles.

Remember to take your time and work in small sections, ensuring that each rhinestone is placed with precision. It's also essential to allow the adhesive or glue to dry completely before handling or wearing your finished project. This prevents any accidental displacement or smudging.

Their sparkling allure and versatility make them an excellent choice for adding a touch of elegance or flair. With the right techniques and materials, you can elevate your crafts to new heights. So go ahead, explore the magical world of rhinestones, and let your creativity shine!.

- Different Types of Rhinestones

1. Flatback Rhinestones:
   Flatback rhinestones are a common choice for DIY enthusiasts. As the name suggests, these rhinestones have a flat back, making them easy to adhere to various surfaces. They come in various shapes, such as round, oval, square, and teardrop, providing versatility for your projects. .

When working with flatback rhinestones, you will need a reliable adhesive. Craft glues or specialized rhinestone glues work best for securing flatback rhinestones to your crafts. Apply a small amount of adhesive to the back of the rhinestone, carefully place it on your desired surface, and press firmly. Allow the adhesive to dry as per the manufacturer's instructions.

2. Sew-On Rhinestones:

As the name suggests, sew-on rhinestones are designed for stitching onto fabric or other materials. These rhinestones come with holes on either end, allowing you to easily sew them onto your projects. Sew-on rhinestones are available in a wide range of colors, sizes, and shapes, making them perfect for adding a touch of glamour to garments, accessories, and home decor items.

When working with sew-on rhinestones, choose a thread that matches the color of your rhinestones and carefully hand or machine-stitch them onto your project. Ensure that you secure the rhinestones adequately to avoid any loosening or falling off.

3. Hotfix Rhinestones:

Hotfix rhinestones have a special adhesive on the back which melts when heat is applied. These rhinestones are popular for creating intricate and detailed designs without the need for glue. A hotfix applicator or a household iron can be used to attach them to various surfaces.

To use hotfix rhinestones, preheat your hotfix applicator or iron to the recommended temperature. Place the rhinestone onto your desired surface, apply heat with the applicator or iron, and gently press down. Hold it in place for a few seconds to ensure the adhesive bonds properly. Allow the rhinestones to cool completely before handling.

4. Resin Rhinestones:

Resin rhinestones are created by pouring a specialized resin mixture into molds, resulting in a three-dimensional and high-shine embellishment. These rhinestones are available in various shapes, such as hearts, flowers, and stars, adding a unique touch to your crafts.

To use resin rhinestones, you will need a strong adhesive such as E6000. Apply a small amount of adhesive to the back of the rhinestone and carefully attach it to your project. Press firmly to ensure a secure bond. Allow the adhesive to dry thoroughly before handling.

Experimenting with Different Rhinestones:

For example, combining flatback and sew-on rhinestones can create an interesting texture on fabric or other surfaces. Don't be afraid to play with different sizes, colors, and shapes to achieve the desired effect.

Remember, the key to successful rhinestone application is to ensure they are properly secured. Whether you choose to use adhesive, stitching, or heat, make sure the bond is strong enough to withstand normal wear and tear.

So, unleash your creativity and get ready to elevate your DIY projects with the magic of rhinestones. With their sparkle and shine, they are sure to make your crafts stand out and leave a lasting impression.

- Rhinestone Crafts Ideas

Rhinestones are fabulous additions to your crafts, adding a touch of glamour and sparkle to any project. This guide will provide you with detailed instructions and inspiration on how to incorporate rhinestones into your DIY paper crafts.

When it comes to DIY paper crafts, the possibilities are endless. With rhinestones, you can take your projects to a whole new level. So let's explore different ideas on how to use rhinestones in your creations.

Rhinestone Monogram Cards:

1. Start with a blank cardstock or card base of your choice. Choose a color that complements the rhinestones you have.

2. Cut out a letter or a monogram shape from a contrasting colored paper. This could be the initial of the recipient's name or a design that holds special meaning.

3. Apply a thin layer of craft glue on the paper letter or monogram shape.

4. Carefully place rhinestones of various sizes and colors on the glued surface. You can create patterns or cover the entire shape with rhinestones, depending on your desired effect.

5. Allow the glue to dry completely before handling the card. Make sure all the rhinestones are firmly secured.

Rhinestone Paper Flowers:

1. Start by cutting out flower shapes from colored or patterned paper. You can use templates or freestyle.

2. Apply a dab of glue in the center of each flower and place a single rhinestone there.

3. Alternatively, you can create a pattern of rhinestones on the petals of the paper flowers.

4. Layer the paper flowers on top of each other, staggering the petals to create depth.

5. Secure the layers with glue or a brad in the center.

Rhinestone Faux Calligraphy:

1. Write or trace a word or phrase on a piece of cardstock or paper using a marker or pen.

2. Apply a thin line of glue along the outline of each letter.

3. Place rhinestones of similar size and color along the glued lines, following the shape of the letters.

4. Let the glue dry completely before handling the finished piece.

Rhinestone Gift Tags:

1. Cut out gift tag shapes from thick cardstock or paper.

2. Punch a hole at the top of each tag to add string or ribbon later.

3. Apply a thin layer of glue on the surface of the tag.

4. Arrange rhinestones in different patterns or shapes on the glued surface.

5. Once the rhinestones are in place, let the glue dry thoroughly before attaching the tags to your gifts.

Rhinestone Bookmarks:

1. Cut out a strip of cardstock or heavy paper to the desired width and length of your bookmark.

2. Apply a thin layer of glue on one side of the bookmark.

3. Arrange rhinestones in a pattern or simply place them randomly on the glued surface.

4. Let the glue dry completely before using the bookmark.

These are just a few ideas to get you started with your DIY Rhinestone Crafts. The key is to let your creativity and imagination run wild. Experiment with different paper shapes, sizes, and colors, and combine them with rhinestones to create unique and eye-catching designs.

Remember to choose rhinestones of various sizes, colors, and finishes to add depth and dimension to your projects. Incorporating rhinestones into your DIY paper crafts will give them a touch of elegance and glamor that will surely impress.

Keep exploring and experimenting with rhinestones to discover even more exciting ways to embellish your crafts. Don't be afraid to think outside the box and try new techniques. Happy crafting!.

Chapter 5: Gemstones

- Introduction to Gemstones

Gemstones are a captivating addition to any DIY project, infusing a touch of glamour and luxury into your creations. In this chapter, we will delve into the world of gemstones, exploring their various types, characteristics, and how they can be incorporated into your embellishments. So, let's embark on this journey of gemstone exploration and discover the endless possibilities they hold for your crafts.

Gemstones come in a wide range of colors, shapes, and sizes, making them a versatile choice for embellishments. From vibrant turquoise to sparkling diamonds, the beauty of gemstones lies in their natural allure. Each gemstone is unique, carrying its own inherent charm and symbolism. Whether you're looking to add a pop of color, a touch of elegance, or a symbol of luck and protection, gemstones can be just the thing to make your DIY creations shine.

To start our exploration, let's understand the different types of gemstones that you can utilize in your crafts. Some popular gemstones include amethyst, aquamarine, citrine, garnet, opal, peridot, topaz, and ruby, to name just a few. Each of these gemstones possesses its own distinct properties and characteristics, such as hardness, color intensity, and refraction of light. These factors contribute to the visual appeal of the gemstones and should be taken into consideration when selecting them for your projects.

When incorporating gemstones into your DIY crafts, there are various ways to go about it. You can directly attach them to your project using adhesive, thread, or wire, depending on the desired effect. Another option is to create settings or bezels to hold the gemstones securely in place. This can be done by shaping wire or using pre-made bezels that can be easily adhered to your project. Whichever method you choose, it's important to ensure a secure and durable attachment to prevent any accidental loss of the gemstones.

In terms of aesthetics, gemstones can be used as standalone embellishments or combined with other materials to create unique designs. For instance, you can create a focal point by placing a single gemstone at the center of a pendant or brooch. Alternatively, you can arrange gemstones in a pattern or design to create a visually appealing effect. Experiment with different combinations and arrangements to find the style that best suits your aesthetic preferences.

Furthermore, gemstones can be combined with other embellishments, such as beads, sequins, and charms, to amplify their visual impact. Mixing textures and materials can create a visually interesting and multidimensional effect. For example, pairing gemstones with beads can add depth and create a luxurious look, while combining gemstones with sequins can add a touch of sparkle and playfulness.

When it comes to sourcing gemstones, there are various options available. You can visit local gemstone and bead shops, browse online marketplaces, or even repurpose old jewelry for their gemstones. Keep in mind that gemstones can vary in price, depending on factors like rarity and quality. It's always a good idea to research and compare prices before making a purchase to ensure you're getting the best value for your money.

Their inherent charm and uniqueness can elevate your creations, adding a touch of sophistication and elegance. Whether used as standalone embellishments or combined with other materials, gemstones offer endless possibilities for creative expression. So, go ahead and explore the world of gemstones, and let your imagination run wild as you incorporate these beautiful gems into your next DIY project.

- Types of Gemstones

Gemstones are a stunning addition to any DIY project, and their beauty and versatility make them a popular choice for embellishments.

One type of gemstone commonly used in DIY projects is the rhinestone. Rhinestones are synthetic gemstones made from crystal or glass that mimic the dazzling sparkle of real jewels. They come in various shapes, sizes, and colors, allowing you to find the perfect rhinestone for your craft. Whether you want to add a touch of glamour to a handbag or create a sparkling design on a picture frame, rhinestones are a fantastic choice.

Another type of gemstone frequently seen in DIY projects is the bead. Beads come in an array of materials, including plastic, glass, wood, and metal. They can be used to add texture, color, and interest to various crafts. Whether you want to create a beaded necklace, embellish a shirt collar, or decorate a scrapbook page, beads offer endless possibilities for creativity.

Gemstones themselves are also a popular choice for DIY embellishments. Natural gemstones, such as amethyst, turquoise, and garnet, can add a touch of elegance and sophistication to any craft project. From adorning a picture frame to creating unique jewelry pieces, gemstones are sure to make a statement.

When it comes to attaching gemstones to your crafts, there are several options to consider. Craft glue or adhesive dots are common choices and provide a secure hold. For fabric-based projects, you can use fabric glue or sew the gemstones onto the material using a needle and thread. It's important to select an adhesive that is compatible with the materials you are working with to ensure a long-lasting bond.

It's essential to keep in mind that gemstones can vary in quality and price. If you are looking for more affordable options, synthetic gemstones or glass crystals can provide a similar look at a fraction of the cost. However, if you are seeking a truly luxurious and high-end finish, investing in genuine gemstones may be the way to go.

When working with gemstones, it's crucial to handle them with care. Be cautious not to drop or mishandle them, as they can crack or break. Additionally, be mindful of the adhesive you use to attach them, as some gemstones may react unfavorably to certain types of glue or adhesive.

Whether you choose rhinestones, beads, or natural gemstones, these embellishments will undoubtedly elevate your crafts to the next level. Remember to choose the right adhesive, handle the gemstones with care, and consider your budget and preferences when selecting the type of gemstone to use. Get creative and have fun with your DIY embellishments using gemstones!.

- Gemstone Crafts Ideas

Gemstones add a touch of elegance and sophistication to any craft project. With their vibrant colors and unique properties, gemstones can truly elevate your DIY creations. From jewelry to home decor, there is no limit to the possibilities. So, let's dive in and unleash your creativity!.

When it comes to DIY paper crafts, gemstones can be a fantastic addition. The iridescent shine of sequins can make your paper crafts fun and eye-catching. You can use sequins to create beautiful greeting cards, embellish gift tags, or even add a touch of sparkle to your scrapbooking projects. Simply glue the sequins onto the paper using a clear adhesive. Experiment with different colors and shapes to create stunning effects.

Beads are another versatile gemstone that can be used in a wide range of crafts. From bracelets and necklaces to keychains and bookmarks, the possibilities are endless. You can string beads together to create intricate patterns or use them as accents on larger projects. To incorporate beads into your DIY paper crafts, you can create beaded borders or even 3D bead designs. Just make sure to use a strong adhesive to secure the beads in place.

Rhinestones are perfect for adding a touch of glamour to your crafts. Their sparkling appearance can instantly transform ordinary items into dazzling pieces of art. In DIY paper crafts, you can use rhinestones to highlight specific elements or create a stunning border around your design. Consider using different sizes and colors of rhinestones to add depth and variation to your projects.

Gemstones themselves can be the centerpiece of your craft projects. Whether you are creating jewelry, home decor, or accessories, gemstones can become the focal point. You can use gemstones as charms on bracelets or pendants on necklaces. For home decor, you can embed gemstones into candle holders, create mosaic patterns on picture frames, or even make gemstone coasters. The only limit is your imagination!.

Pom-poms, feathers, and felt are other materials that can be combined with gemstones to create unique crafts. For instance, you can attach gemstones to pom-poms to make adorable keychains or attach them to feathers to create fancy feather pens. Felt can be used as a backing for gemstone jewelry or as a base for gemstone hair accessories. The soft texture of these materials complements the sparkle of gemstones beautifully.

Cork is another material that pairs well with gemstones in DIY crafts. You can create gemstone pushpins for your bulletin board or coasters with gemstone accents. The natural texture and color of cork add a rustic feel to your projects, making them stand out even more.

If you're looking to incorporate gemstones into your crafts beyond paper and fabric, tapes can be a great option. Washi tape, fabric tape, duct tape, and masking tape can all be embellished with gemstones to create unique designs. You can decorate notebooks, phone cases, and even furniture with gemstone-adorned tapes. The adhesive on these tapes allows for easy application and removal, making it a fun and versatile option.

Lastly, glitter, glitter glue, sequin waste, tinsel, and foil can all be used in conjunction with gemstones to add sparkle and shine to your creations. Whether you want to create a whimsical greeting card, a sparkling Christmas ornament, or a glamorous jewelry piece, these materials can help you achieve the desired effect.

Remember, when working with gemstones, always use a strong adhesive to ensure they stay in place. You can find a variety of adhesives specifically designed for gemstone crafting at your local craft store. Also, don't be afraid to mix and match different types of gemstones to create a truly unique look.

Whether you're a beginner or an experienced DIY enthusiast, these ideas will surely take your projects to the next level. So grab your gemstones and get crafting!.

Chapter 6: Charms

- Introduction to Charms

In the fascinating world of DIY crafts, charms are a delightful addition that can beautifully complement your projects. These small decorative trinkets have the power to enhance any creation, making it truly unique and personal. In this chapter, we will delve into the enchanting realm of charms, exploring their various types and providing step-by-step instructions on how to incorporate them into your DIY crafts.

Buttons, sequins, beads, rhinestones, gemstones, charms, pom-poms, feathers, felt, cork, washi tape, fabric tape, duct tape, masking tape, glitter, glitter glue, sequin waste, tinsel, foil, and aluminum foil – these are just a few of the many materials available for your charm-making endeavors. Each of these materials opens up a whole new realm of creativity and possibilities.

When it comes to creating charms using buttons, you have virtually endless options. Buttons come in all shapes, sizes, and colors, allowing you to choose ones that perfectly align with the aesthetic you wish to achieve. To create a button charm, start by selecting your desired button and ensuring that it has a loop or hole to attach it to your crafts. You can then use an open jump ring or a piece of thin wire to attach the button to your desired project.

Sequins, on the other hand, offer a touch of sparkle and glamour to your DIY crafts. Whether you want to create a sequin charm to add a pop of color to a handmade accessory or to embellish a greeting card, the process is fairly straightforward. Begin by threading your chosen sequin onto a piece of jewellery wire or thread. Secure the sequin in place by making a knot or using a small crimp bead. Lastly, attach your sequin charm to your desired project using a jump ring or wire loop.

Beads are yet another charming addition to your creations and come in an astonishing variety of shapes, sizes, and materials. To make a bead charm, simply string your chosen beads onto a headpin or eyepin, leaving a small loop at the end. Attach the charm to your project using a jump ring or wire loop.

Similarly, rhinestones and gemstones can add a touch of elegance and sophistication to your DIY crafts. The process of creating a charm with these materials involves using wire or thread to secure the stone in place, giving it a loop to be easily attached to your project.

Pom-poms, feathers, felt, and cork charms bring a tactile and whimsical element to your crafts. These materials can be easily shaped and attached to your projects using glue or a small wire loop.

For those who love working with tapes, washi tape, fabric tape, duct tape, and masking tape can be used to create unique charms. Simply cut or tear off a small section of tape, fold it in on itself, and secure it with a jump ring or wire loop.

When it comes to adding a touch of sparkle, glitter and glitter glue are excellent choices. Apply a thin layer of glue onto your chosen surface and sprinkle the glitter over it. Shake off any excess glitter and allow it to dry. To attach a glitter charm to your project, create a loop using wire or jump rings.

Other materials like sequin waste, tinsel, foil, and aluminum foil provide more unconventional options for your charm-making endeavors. You can shape these materials into interesting forms, secure them with glue or wire, and attach them to your crafts.

Whether you prefer buttons, sequins, beads, or any other material listed, the possibilities are truly endless. Enhance your crafts, express your unique style, and let your creativity shine with these captivating charms.

- Different Types of Charms

Charms are wonderful additions to any DIY project, bringing a touch of personality and character. There are various types of charms that you can create using different materials, allowing you to customize your crafts to suit your preferences and style. In this guide, I will provide detailed instructions on how to make charms using various materials such as paper crafts, buttons, sequins, beads, rhinestones, gemstones, pom-poms, feathers, felt, cork, washi tape, fabric tape, duct tape, masking tape, glitter, glitter glue, sequin waste, tinsel, foil, and aluminum foil.

Let's start with DIY Paper Crafts for making charms. Paper charms can be created in different shapes and sizes using various techniques. To make a paper charm, begin by selecting the desired paper material. It could be scrapbook paper, origami paper, or even plain colored paper that you can personalize with your own designs. Cut out the desired shape for your charm, such as a heart, star, or any other shape that appeals to you. Once the shape is ready, you can further embellish it by adding patterns, colors, or even metallic accents using paints, markers, or glitter. Finally, attach a small loop, made from thread or thin wire, to the top of the charm to create a loop for hanging or attaching it to your DIY projects.

Moving on to button charms, buttons can provide a vintage or quirky touch to your crafts. To make a button charm, start by selecting a button of your choice. It could be a single-colored button, a patterned one, or even one with a unique shape. If you want to add more variety, consider combining multiple buttons in different sizes and shapes. To attach the buttons together and create a charm, you can use various techniques. One option is to sew them together using a strong thread, making sure to secure each button firmly. Alternatively, you can use glue or adhesive tape to attach the buttons together. Once the buttons are securely attached, you can further enhance the charm by adding small embellishments like beads, sequins, or rhinestones to give it a more glamorous look.

Sequin charms are another fascinating option that adds sparkle to your crafts. To make sequin charms, start with a base material like felt or fabric in your chosen shape, such as a circle, star, or flower. Secure the sequins onto the base material using a needle and thread, ensuring that they are tightly stitched to prevent them from falling off. You can create various patterns and combinations with different colored sequins to make unique and vibrant charms. Once the sequins are attached, finish off the charm by adding a loop or finding at the top for easy attachment to your DIY projects.

Bead charms are versatile and offer endless possibilities for customization. To make bead charms, you will need a stringing material like nylon thread or jewelry wire along with various beads of your choice. Begin by cutting a suitable length of thread or wire, considering the desired size of your charm. Thread the beads onto the stringing material in your preferred pattern, alternating colors, shapes, and sizes to create the desired effect. Once all the beads are strung, tie the ends securely to form a loop or attach a jump ring for easy attachment.

Rhinestone and gemstone charms provide an elegant and dazzling touch to your crafts. To make these charms, you will need rhinestones or gemstones of your choice, along with strong adhesive or jewelry glue. Apply a small amount of adhesive to the back of each rhinestone or gemstone and carefully place it onto a base material, such as metal, plastic, or fabric. Allow the adhesive to dry completely before using the charm in your DIY projects.

Pom-pom charms bring a fun and playful element to your crafts. To make pom-pom charms, you can use store-bought pom-poms or create your own by wrapping yarn around a piece of cardboard and securing it in the middle with a separate piece of yarn. Once the pom-pom is formed, attach a loop or finding to the center of the pom-pom using a thread or wire. This will ensure that the charm can be easily attached to your projects.

Feather charms add a touch of nature and delicacy to your crafts. To create feather charms, start with a set of feathers in various shapes and sizes. Trim the feathers to the desired length, making sure to remove any excess materials or sharp edges. Attach a loop or finding to the top of each feather using a small piece of wire or thread, creating a loop for attaching the charm to your DIY projects.

Felt charms allow you to experiment with different shapes and textures. To make felt charms, cut out pieces of felt in your desired shape and size. You can opt for simple shapes like hearts, circles, or stars, or get creative with more intricate designs. Attach a loop or finding to the top of the felt charm using a thread or wire, ensuring that it is securely fastened for easy attachment to your crafts.

Cork charms offer a unique and organic touch to your creations. To make cork charms, you can either use pre-cut cork shapes or cut your own from natural cork sheets. Sand the edges of the cork pieces to smooth them out if needed. Attach a loop or finding to the top of each cork charm using a small piece of wire or thread, allowing for easy attachment to your DIY projects.

Washi tape, fabric tape, duct tape, and masking tape charms provide a DIY and colorful option for your crafts. To make these charms, simply cut a small piece of the chosen tape and fold it onto itself, creating a loop or a folded shape. Secure the ends by pressing them together, ensuring they are firmly attached. You can further enhance the charm by adding small embellishments like buttons, beads, or rhinestones.

Glitter and glitter glue charms add a touch of sparkle to your crafts. To make these charms, start by cutting out a shape from a sturdy material like cardboard or thin plastic. Apply a layer of glue onto the surface of the shape and sprinkle glitter over it, making sure to cover the entire surface evenly. Shake off any excess glitter and allow the glue to dry completely before attaching a loop or finding for easy attachment.

Sequin waste, tinsel, foil, and aluminum foil charms allow you to reuse and upcycle materials for a unique look. To make these charms, cut out pieces of the desired material in your chosen shape, ensuring that it is sturdy enough to hold its shape. Attach a loop or finding to the top of the charm using a small piece of wire or thread, allowing for easy attachment to your DIY projects.

Whether it's paper crafts, buttons, sequins, beads, rhinestones, gemstones, pom-poms, feathers, felt, cork, washi tape, fabric tape, duct tape, masking tape, glitter, glitter glue, sequin waste, tinsel, foil, or aluminum foil, each charm can be customized to suit your preferences and style. By following the instructions in this guide, you can easily create charming and unique embellishments for all your crafting endeavors. Happy crafting!.

- Charm Crafts Ideas

In this chapter, we will explore the wonderful world of charm crafts using various materials like buttons, sequins, beads, rhinestones, gemstones, charms, pom-poms, feathers, felt, cork, washi tape, fabric tape, duct tape, masking tape, glitter, glitter glue, sequin waste, tinsel, foil, and aluminum foil. These materials offer endless opportunities to create unique and personalized charm crafts that can be used for various purposes like jewelry, keychains, home decor, and more.

Buttons, often overlooked, can be a fantastic material for charm crafts. You can create adorable button charm bracelets or necklaces by stringing buttons of different sizes and colors onto an elastic string. You can mix and match buttons to create unique patterns and add a touch of individuality to your accessory. Alternatively, you can attach a small loop to the back of a button and turn it into a cute button charm for a zipper pull or as a decorative element on a bookmark or greeting card.

Sequins are another versatile material that can add a touch of sparkle to your charm crafts. You can create beautiful sequin charms by stitching or gluing sequins onto a felt or fabric base in various shapes like hearts, stars, or animals. These sequin charms can be used as pendants, earrings, or even as embellishments on clothing, bags, or shoes. With a little creativity, you can combine different sizes and colors of sequins to create stunning designs that will catch everyone's eye.

Beads are perhaps one of the most popular materials for charm crafts. They come in various shapes, sizes, and materials, allowing you to explore endless possibilities. You can create charm bracelets or necklaces by stringing beads onto a wire or elastic cord. Mix different types of beads like glass, wooden, or acrylic, and add some charms or pendants to make your creations truly unique. Don't forget to experiment with different color combinations to create eye-catching designs.

Rhinestones and gemstones are perfect for adding a touch of elegance and glamour to your charm crafts. You can use flat-back rhinestones to create sparkling accents on your charm creations, or glue faceted gemstones onto a base to create stunning pendants or brooches. These charms can be used to dress up your accessories or to add a touch of sparkle to your home decor items.

Charms, as the name suggests, are in themselves little works of art. You can create your own charms using various materials like polymer clay, metal, or resin. Simply shape the material into your desired charm design, bake or set it according to the material's instructions, and voila - you have a unique charm ready to be used in your crafts. Charms can be attached to jewelry, keychains, or used as zipper pulls, giving a personal touch to your creations.

Pom-poms, feathers, felt, and cork can add a playful and textural element to your charm crafts. You can create cute charms by attaching small pom-poms or feathers to a base, or cut shapes out of felt or cork and decorate them with paints, markers, or other embellishments. These charms can be used on crafts like bookmarks, hair accessories, or even as decorative elements on greeting cards or gift wrap.

Washi tape, fabric tape, duct tape, masking tape, and glitter can all be used to add color, pattern, and texture to your charm crafts. Use these tapes to cover a base or create various shapes and designs. You can also use glitter or glitter glue to add a touch of sparkle and shine to your charm creations. The possibilities are endless, and you can easily customize your charms to match your own personal style.

Sequin waste, tinsel, foil, and aluminum foil may not be the first materials that come to mind for charm crafts, but they can add unique and unexpected elements to your creations. Sequin waste, which is the leftover material from sequin production, can be used to add texture and shine to your charms. Tinsel, foil, and aluminum foil can be shaped and transformed into unique charms that can be used in various crafts.

Whether you choose to work with buttons, sequins, beads, rhinestones, gemstones, charms, pom-poms, feathers, felt, cork, washi tape, fabric tape, duct tape, masking tape, glitter, glitter glue, sequin waste, tinsel, foil, or aluminum foil, you can unleash your creativity and create personalized charm crafts that reflect your own individual style. So, grab your favorite materials and start crafting!.

Chapter 7: Pom-poms

- Introduction to Pom-poms

Pom-poms are a fun and versatile embellishment that can add a touch of creativity and playfulness to all sorts of DIY projects. Whether you're making accessories, home decor items, or clothing, pom-poms can be an excellent addition. In this chapter, we will explore how to create pom-poms, the various materials you can use, and the techniques involved in DIY pom-pom making.

To begin with, let's discuss the materials you'll need for making pom-poms. Depending on your preferences and the desired outcome, you can choose from a range of materials. From traditional yarn to more unconventional options like paper or fabric, the possibilities are limitless. Some common materials used for making pom-poms include paper crafts, buttons, sequins, beads, rhinestones, gemstones, charms, feathers, felt, cork, washi tape, fabric tape, duct tape, masking tape, glitter, glitter glue, sequin waste, tinsel, foil, and even aluminum foil.

When it comes to DIY paper crafts for pom-poms, the process is relatively simple. Start by cutting multiple strips of paper in the desired length and width. The length of the paper determines the fullness of the pom-pom, so experiment until you achieve the desired effect. Next, stack the paper strips on top of each other, keeping them aligned at one end. Hold the stack securely and begin folding accordion-style, making sure to maintain consistency in each fold. Once the entire stack is folded, secure it in the middle with a string, thread, or a small binder clip. Finally, unravel the folded paper, fluffing it up gently, and your DIY paper pom-pom is ready to be used as an embellishment.

When working with materials like buttons, sequins, beads, rhinestones, gemstones, charms, feathers, felt, or cork, the process is slightly different. Start by choosing the appropriate size and style of material for your pom-pom. Depending on the desired outcome, you can opt for uniform or eclectic designs. Attach the chosen materials to a foam or fabric base using a strong adhesive. Make sure to cover the entire surface evenly, ensuring that no gaps are left. Allow the adhesive to dry completely before handling or attaching the pom-pom to your project.

In addition to the mentioned materials, you can also experiment with different types of tapes such as washi tape, fabric tape, duct tape, and masking tape to create unique pom-pom designs. These tapes can be wrapped around foam or fabric bases in various patterns and colors, enabling you to showcase your creativity. Additionally, you can incorporate glitter, glitter glue, sequin waste, tinsel, and foil into your pom-pom creations to add sparkle and dimension.

When it comes to working with aluminum foil, the process requires a slightly different approach. Start by cutting strips of aluminum foil in the desired length and width. Similar to the paper pom-poms, stack the foil strips on top of each other and fold accordion-style. Secure the folded foil stack in the middle and then fluff it up gently to create your shiny and reflective pom-pom.

By using a variety of materials such as paper crafts, buttons, sequins, beads, and more, you can customize your pom-poms to suit any occasion or style. Whether you're embellishing accessories, home decor items, or clothing, pom-poms are a delightful way to add a touch of whimsy and charm to your projects. So, gather your materials, unleash your imagination, and start crafting your own unique pom-poms today!.

- Types of Pom-poms

Pom-poms are versatile and charming embellishments that can elevate the look of any craft project. Whether you are creating accessories, home decor, or even clothing, pom-poms can add a touch of whimsy and playfulness.

To start off, let's look at paper pom-poms. These are easy to make and require minimal supplies. Cut strips of paper in desired widths, and make accordion folds along the length of the strip. Fold it in half and secure the center with a piece of string or wire. Carefully separate each layer and fluff it up to create a pom-pom shape. You can experiment with different colors and sizes to add a vibrant element to your DIY projects.

Sequins can also be used to create unique pom-poms. Thread sequins onto a string or wire in a pattern that you prefer. Gather them at one end and secure with a knot. Fluff them up, and you have a dazzling sequin pom-pom. This technique works exceptionally well when creating accessories, such as a keychain or a hair accessory.

Beads are another fantastic option for pom-pom creation. Choose beads in various shapes, sizes, and colors. Thread them onto a long piece of wire, leaving a small gap at the ends. Gather the beads together and twist the wire tightly to secure them. Gently fluff up the beads to form a pom-pom that exudes elegance and sophistication.

For a more glamorous touch, rhinestone pom-poms are a perfect choice. Using a similar technique to the sequin pom-poms, thread rhinestones onto a string or wire. Combine different sizes and colors to create a mesmerizing effect. Gather them together and secure them tightly. Once again, fluff up the rhinestones to create a dazzling and eye-catching pom-pom.

Gemstones can also be utilized to create stunning pom-poms. Select gemstones in various colors and shapes. Attach them to a base, such as a large bead or a metal ring, using a strong adhesive. Arrange the gemstones closely together to create a dense pom-pom. This type of pom-pom is perfect for adding a touch of luxury to decorative items like curtains or lampshades.

Moving on to charms, they can provide a delightful element in your DIY pom-poms. Choose charms that resonate with the theme or purpose of your project. Secure them to a string or a chain and gather them together. Fluff them up and watch your pom-pom come to life with imaginative and whimsical charm.

Feathers can lend an ethereal and dreamy feel to your pom-poms. Gather a selection of feathers in various colors and sizes. Secure them to a base, such as a Styrofoam ball or a wooden bead, using hot glue. Spread the feathers out to create a full-bodied and enchanting pom-pom. This type of pom-pom works remarkably well when adorning headbands or handbags.

For a softer texture, felt pom-poms can be a delightful option. Cut felt sheets into small squares or circles. Fold each square or circle into quarters and secure the center with a stitch. Repeat this process with several felt pieces. Gather them together and sew them tightly. Fluff up the felt layers gently, and you will have a cozy and visually pleasing felt pom-pom.

Cork pom-poms are unique and add a touch of rustic charm to your projects. Cut thin strips of cork and roll them up, securing with a dab of hot glue. Repeat this process with multiple cork strips. Gather them together and secure tightly. Gently separate and shape the cork strips to create a whimsical and eco-friendly pom-pom.

The possibilities with pom-pom creations are endless, and the options mentioned above are just scratching the surface. I hope this detailed guide has inspired you to embark on your own pom-pom journey. Experiment with various materials, colors, and techniques to bring your DIY projects to life. Enjoy the process and let your creativity soar as you embellish your crafts with unique and wonderful pom-poms.

- Pom-pom Crafts Ideas

Pom-poms are a versatile embellishment that can be used in various DIY crafts to add a touch of fun and style. In this chapter, we will explore some exciting and creative ideas for incorporating pom-poms into your crafts. Whether you're a seasoned DIY enthusiast or a beginner looking to try something new, these pom-pom craft ideas are sure to inspire you.

Pom-poms can be made from many different materials, including yarn, fabric, and even tissue paper. One of the most common ways to create pom-poms is by using yarn. To make a yarn pom-pom, you'll need a few supplies such as yarn, scissors, and a pom-pom maker. .

Here's a simple step-by-step guide to creating a yarn pom-pom:

1. Start by wrapping the yarn around the pom-pom maker. The more times you wrap the yarn, the fuller and fluffier your pom-pom will be.

2. Once you've wrapped the yarn around the pom-pom maker to your desired thickness, use the scissors to cut the yarn.

3. Carefully remove the wrapped yarn from the pom-pom maker.

4. Take a separate piece of yarn and tie it tightly around the middle of the wrapped yarn. This will secure the pom-pom in place.

5. Use the scissors to cut the loops on both sides of the pom-pom. This will create the pom-pom shape.

6. Give your pom-pom a little trim to even out the edges and make it look neat.

Now that you know how to create basic yarn pom-poms, let's explore some DIY craft ideas where you can use them.

1. Pom-pom garland: Create a beautiful garland by stringing yarn pom-poms onto a string or ribbon. You can alternate different colors and sizes of pom-poms to make it more visually appealing. Hang the garland on your walls, mantel, or even use it as party decor.

2. Pom-pom keychains: Add a pop of color to your keys or bags by attaching pom-poms to key rings. You can mix and match different colors and sizes to create a unique keychain that reflects your style.

3. Pom-pom bookmarks: Make reading even more enjoyable with cute pom-pom bookmarks. Simply attach a small pom-pom to the end of a ribbon or string and place it between the pages of your favorite book.

4. Pom-pom earrings: Get creative with pom-pom earrings by attaching small pom-poms to earring hooks. You can make a statement with bright and bold colored pom-poms or keep it simple with neutral tones. Either way, these earrings are sure to catch attention.

5. Pom-pom wreath: Create a festive wreath for any occasion by attaching pom-poms to a foam wreath form. You can choose pom-poms in colors that match the theme or decor of your event. Add some ribbon or bow for a finishing touch.

These are just a few ideas to get you started with pom-pom crafts. The possibilities are endless, and you can let your creativity shine by incorporating pom-poms into various DIY projects. Experiment with different materials, sizes, and colors to create unique and personalized crafts that will impress everyone.

Remember, pom-poms are not only fun to make, but they also add a touch of whimsy and vibrancy to any craft project. So, grab your supplies and start creating beautiful pom-pom crafts today!.

Chapter 8: Feathers

- Introduction to Feathers

Feathers have long been a popular choice for embellishments in crafting projects. Their natural beauty and delicate nature can add a touch of elegance and whimsy to any DIY creation. In this chapter, we will explore the world of feathers and delve into various techniques and ideas for incorporating them into your designs.

When it comes to using feathers in your crafts, the possibilities are truly endless. Feathers can be used in a wide array of projects, from jewelry and accessories to home décor and clothing embellishments. They can be combined with other materials such as buttons, sequins, beads, rhinestones, gemstones, charms, pom-poms, felt, cork, washi tape, fabric tape, duct tape, masking tape, glitter, glitter glue, sequin waste, tinsel, foil, and even aluminum foil.

Before you begin working with feathers, it's important to understand the different types and sizes available. Feathers come in various shapes and sizes, each with its own unique characteristics. Some common types of feathers include ostrich feathers, peacock feathers, marabou feathers, and hackle feathers. Ostrich feathers are large and dramatic, while peacock feathers are known for their iridescent colors. Marabou feathers are fluffy and delicate, and hackle feathers have a stiffer appearance.

To start incorporating feathers into your crafts, you will need a few essential tools and materials. First and foremost, you will need to source high-quality feathers. Ensure that the feathers are clean, undamaged, and free from any unwanted odors. You can find feathers at craft stores, online retailers, or even by repurposing materials from old clothing or accessories.

To attach feathers to your projects, you will need some adhesive. A good option is to use a glue gun, as it provides a strong bond and dries quickly. Alternatively, you can use craft glue or even sew feathers directly onto fabric or other materials.

When working with feathers, it's crucial to handle them with care. Feathers are delicate and can easily be damaged if mishandled. Always wash your hands before touching feathers to prevent any oils from transferring onto them. Additionally, avoid exposing feathers to excessive heat or moisture, as this can cause them to lose their shape or become discolored.

Feathers can be used in a variety of ways to enhance your crafts. For jewelry and accessories, you can create feather earrings, necklaces, or even hair clips. You can also incorporate feathers into your home décor by adding them to wreaths, floral arrangements, or wall hangings. Feathers can also be used to embellish clothing items such as hats, jackets, or handbags.

To add dimension to your crafts, consider combining feathers with other materials such as beads, sequins, or rhinestones. This will create a stunning visual impact and make your projects truly stand out. Experiment with different color combinations and layering techniques to achieve the desired effect.

Whether you're a novice or a seasoned crafter, incorporating feathers into your designs is sure to elevate your creations to a whole new level. Remember to handle feathers with care, choose high-quality materials, and explore various techniques to unleash your creativity. So go ahead, let your imagination take flight and start crafting with feathers today!.

- Different Types of Feathers

Feathers are a versatile and captivating material that can be used in various crafting projects, from costumes to home decor. In this chapter, we will specifically delve into the world of feather crafts.

Feathers come in a wide range of shapes, sizes, and colors, and it's essential to understand their characteristics before you embark on a feather crafting journey. Ostrich feathers, for example, are large and feathery, making them ideal for dramatic fashion statements. On the other hand, goose feathers are smaller and more delicate, lending themselves beautifully to dreamcatchers or hair accessories. It is crucial to choose the right feathers for your project to achieve the desired effect.

Once you have gathered the feathers you need, there are various techniques you can employ to manipulate them and bring them to life. The first technique is simply using feathers as they are, maintaining their natural appearance. This works well if you want to create a realistic effect or add a touch of nature to your project. You can attach these feathers to any surface or item using glue, stitching, or wire.

Another technique to consider is dyeing or painting the feathers. This allows you to expand your color palette and create feathers that match your project perfectly. To dye feathers, you can use fabric dye or watercolor paints. Dip your feathers into the dye or paint mixture, making sure to evenly distribute the color. Allow them to dry completely before using them in your craft. Keep in mind that it's best to test the dye or paint on a small portion of the feather before committing to the entire batch.

If you want to add texture or dimension to your feathers, you can try cutting, curling, or combing them. With a pair of sharp scissors, carefully trim the edges of the feathers to create different shapes, such as rounded, oval, or jagged-edged feathers. This offers a unique visual appeal and can be used to create intricate patterns or designs. Curling feathers involves gently heating them with a hairdryer, steam, or hot water, and then shaping them while they are still pliable. This technique works particularly well for creating feathered motifs or ornaments. Additionally, combing feathers with a fine-toothed comb can make them look fluffy and well-groomed, perfect for birds' wings or hair accessories.

Moreover, combining feathers with other materials can create breathtaking effects. For example, incorporating beads, sequins, or rhinestones can add sparkle and glamour to your feathered creations. Attach these embellishments with glue or stitching, being mindful of the weight and size of the feathers you are using. Additionally, consider layering feathers to create depth and visual interest. Experiment with arranging feathers of different lengths and colors to achieve stunning effects.

Feathers can also be combined with fabric, felt, or paper to create unique textures and patterns. For example, attaching feathers to fabric with glue or stitching can produce a whimsical and bohemian look. Adding feathers to felt or paper backgrounds can create eye-catching cards or wall art. The possibilities are endless; let your creativity guide you.

Lastly, it is essential to take proper care of your feather crafts to ensure their longevity. Avoid exposing them to excessive moisture, direct sunlight, or rough handling. Keep them away from pets or children who may inadvertently damage the feathers. If necessary, gently dust your feather creations with a soft brush or use a blow dryer on a cool setting to remove any built-up dust.

Whether you are using feathers in their natural form, dyeing or painting them, cutting or curling them, or combining them with other materials, the key is to unleash your imagination and let your creativity soar. With a little patience and practice, you will be able to craft stunning feather creations that add beauty and elegance to any project. Happy crafting!.

- Feather Crafts Ideas

Feathers are a fascinating and versatile material that can add a touch of elegance and whimsy to your DIY crafts. In this chapter, we will explore some creative ways to incorporate feathers into your projects.

Feather Wreath:

One idea for using feathers in your crafts is to make a beautiful feather wreath. Start by acquiring a foam wreath form, preferably in the size of your choice. Next, gather an assortment of feathers in different sizes, colors, and textures. You can purchase feathers from a craft store or even use natural feathers from birds if you prefer. Consider arranging the feathers in a gradient pattern, alternating colors and lengths. Secure the feathers to the foam form using glue. Finally, add any additional embellishments such as ribbons, sequins, or beads for a more personalized touch. Hang your feather wreath on a door, wall, or above a mantel to create a stunning focal point in your home.

Feather Earrings:

For those who love to accessorize, feather earrings can be a unique and eye-catching addition to your jewelry collection. To make feather earrings, start by selecting a pair of earring hooks or studs, depending on your preference. Attach a small jump ring to the earring hook or stud. Then, choose a few feathers that match your desired style and trim them to a suitable length. Thread the feathers through the jump ring and secure them. You can also add other elements, such as beads or charms, to enhance the earrings' visual appeal. Be sure to seal the ends of the feathers with clear nail polish or a similar adhesive to prevent fraying. Once the feathers are secured, you can enjoy flaunting your unique feather earrings with pride.

Feather Dreamcatcher:

Another exciting feather craft idea is to make a dreamcatcher adorned with feathers. Traditional Native American dreamcatchers were believed to filter out bad dreams and allow only good dreams to pass through. To create your own feather dreamcatcher, you will need a hoop, suede cord or yarn, feathers, and decorative elements like beads or crystals. Start by wrapping the hoop with the suede cord or yarn, leaving spaces for attaching the feathers later on. Then, tie individual strands of suede cord or yarn to the bottom of the hoop, leaving a few inches of length. Attach feathers to each strand using a simple knot. You can choose feathers in different colors and sizes to add visual interest to your dreamcatcher. Finally, decorate the dreamcatcher with beads or crystals by threading them onto the strands alongside the feathers. Hang your feather dreamcatcher above your bed or in a window to add a touch of bohemian style to your space while warding off bad dreams.

Whether you decide to create a feather wreath, feather earrings, or a feather dreamcatcher, these feather craft ideas will allow your creativity to soar. Challenge yourself to experiment with different types of feathers, colors, and textures to achieve a unique and personalized result in each of your feather crafts. Let your imagination take flight and enjoy crafting with feathers!.

Chapter 9: Felt

- Introduction to Felt

A re you ready to dive into the wonderful world of felt crafting? In this chapter, we will explore the versatile and charming material that is felt. Felt is often overlooked in the DIY world, but its potential for creating beautiful and unique embellishments is truly limitless.

Felt is a textile material that is made by matting together fibers with the help of heat, moisture, and pressure. It has been utilized by humans for centuries due to its durability and versatility. Felt can be made from different types of fibers, such as wool, synthetic materials, or a combination of both. Each type of fiber will result in a slightly different texture and appearance, so it's worth experimenting with different options to find the one that suits your crafting needs.

One of the most common uses of felt in the DIY world is for creating buttons. Felt buttons are not only adorable but also easy to make. All you need is some felt, a button mold, and some basic sewing skills. Simply cut out two circles of felt slightly larger than your button mold, place them in the mold, and sew them together tightly using a coordinating thread. Once you remove the button from the mold, you'll have a perfectly cute and personalized felt button ready to use in your crafting projects.

Sequins, another popular embellishment, can also be easily incorporated into felt crafting. To create sequined felt embellishments, start by cutting out your desired shape from a piece of felt. It can be anything from a simple heart to a more intricate design. Next, choose your sequins and arrange them on the felt in your desired pattern. To secure the sequins in place, simply stitch them onto the felt using a matching thread. The result will be a stunning and eye-catching felt embellishment that can be used in various ways, such as on garments, accessories, or even home decor items.

Beaded felt embellishments offer yet another way to add texture and visual interest to your DIY projects. Start by selecting a piece of felt in your preferred color and cut out your desired shape. Then, choose your beads. They can be different sizes, colors, or even shapes! To attach the beads to the felt, you can use a needle and thread. Simply sew each bead securely onto the felt, creating patterns or designs as you go. The end result will be a lovely beaded felt embellishment that will surely impress anyone who sees it.

Rhinestones, gemstones, and charms can also be incorporated into felt crafting to add a touch of sparkle and elegance. To attach these embellishments securely to your felt, you can either sew them on with a needle and thread or use glue specifically designed for attaching embellishments. Another option is to use hotfix rhinestones or gemstones, which have a heat-activated adhesive on the back. By applying heat with a hotfix applicator or an iron, you can easily adhere them to your felt creations. Just remember to follow the manufacturer's instructions for the specific product you're using.

If you're looking to add a playful and whimsical touch to your craft projects, consider using pom-poms and feathers in combination with felt. Pom-poms can be glued or sewn onto felt, creating a fun and fluffy texture. Feathers, on the other hand, can be attached with glue or neatly sewn onto your felt surface, instantly adding a touch of elegance and movement to your creations.

Now that we've explored some of the ways to incorporate felt into various embellishments, let's talk about the different types of felt that are available. Wool felt is known for being high-quality and dense, making it great for projects that require durability. It is available in a range of colors and is particularly well-suited for creating buttons, brooches, or appliques. Synthetic felt is a more affordable option and comes in a wide array of colors and thicknesses. It is perfect for larger or more budget-friendly projects.

Whether you want to create buttons, sequined embellishments, beaded designs, or even combine it with other materials like pom-poms or feathers, felt offers endless possibilities. Just remember to choose the right type of felt for your project, experiment with different techniques, and most importantly, let your creativity soar. Happy crafting!.

- Types of Felt

Felt is a versatile and widely-used material in the world of DIY crafting. It is known for its soft texture, strength, and ability to be molded into different shapes and designs.

1. Wool Felt:

Wool felt is the most common and popular type of felt used in crafting. It is made from natural sheep's wool and is known for its softness, durability, and ease of use. Wool felt comes in a wide range of colors, making it perfect for creating colorful embellishments or adding detailing to your creations. Its high-quality texture and warmth add an element of elegance to any project.

2. Acrylic/Polyester Felt:

Acrylic or polyester felt is a synthetic alternative to wool felt. It is often used as a more affordable option and is widely available in craft stores. It comes in a variety of colors and has a smooth, shiny surface, which can add a different look and feel to your designs. However, the downside of acrylic or polyester felt is that it is not as durable as wool felt and may not retain its shape as well.

3. Craft Felt:

Craft felt is a general term used to refer to a wide range of felt materials that are specifically designed for crafting purposes. Craft felt can be made from a combination of different fibers, such as wool and synthetic materials, depending on the manufacturer. It is available in a variety of colors, thicknesses, and textures, making it suitable for different types of projects. Craft felt is often the go-to choice for beginners as it is easy to work with and can be found at a reasonable price.

4. Adhesive Felt:

Adhesive felt is a convenient option for those who prefer to skip the hassle of sewing or gluing on felt pieces. Adhesive felt comes with a sticky backing, allowing you to directly attach it to your desired surface. This type of felt is ideal for quick and easy embellishments or for adding a pop of color to different items.

5. Blended Felt:

Blended felt refers to felt that is made from a combination of different fibers or materials. This type of felt is often used when a specific texture or appearance is desired. For example, a blend of wool and polyester can create a sturdier felt with a smoother finish. Blended felt offers versatility and allows for more creative possibilities in your projects.

When working with felt, it is important to consider the quality, thickness, and color of the felt based on your project requirements. Additionally, keep in mind that some felt materials may require special care or additional tools, such as a felting needle for wool felt, to achieve certain designs or techniques.

The choice of felt will greatly impact the overall look and feel of your creations, so don't be afraid to explore and experiment with different felts to achieve the desired effect.

Remember, crafting is all about creativity, and with the right choice of felt, you can add an extra layer of charm and uniqueness to your handmade creations. Happy crafting!.

- Felt Crafts Ideas

Felt is a versatile and tactile material that is perfect for creating a wide range of DIY crafts. Whether you are a beginner or an experienced artisan, working with felt can be a rewarding and enjoyable experience. In this chapter, we will explore some creative ideas and techniques for crafting with felt.

There are numerous options when it comes to DIY felt crafts. You can make anything from simple ornaments and keychains to more elaborate projects like plush toys and home decor items. The possibilities are endless, and with a little bit of imagination and creativity, you can bring your ideas to life.

To get started, you will need a few essential supplies for your felt crafts. These include:

1. Felt: Choose a variety of colors and types of felt, such as wool or acrylic, depending on your preferences and project requirements. Felt sheets or rolls are widely available in craft stores and online.

Now, let's delve into some fun and inspiring felt craft ideas:

1. Felt ornaments: Create adorable ornaments for the holiday season or special occasions. Cut out shapes like snowflakes, hearts, stars, or animals from different colored felt sheets. Embellish them with buttons, sequins, beads, or rhinestones for a festive touch. Attach a loop of ribbon or string for hanging.

2. Felt plush toys: Make cute stuffed animals or dolls using felt. Cut out two identical shapes for the front and back of the toy, then sew them together, leaving a small opening for stuffing. Fill the toy with polyester fiberfill or cotton, and sew the opening closed. Use embroidery floss or felt scraps to add eyes, noses, and other details.

3. Felt flowers: Create lovely fabric flowers with felt. Cut out petal shapes from different colored felt sheets, then stack and layer them to form a flower. Secure the layers with fabric glue or hand stitching. Add a button or bead to the center for an extra touch of elegance.

4. Felt brooches: Design stylish brooches using felt as a base. Cut out a shape, such as a heart or a flower, from felt, and decorate it with sequins, beads,

or rhinestones. Attach a brooch pin or a bar pin to the back using fabric glue or stitching. Wear the brooch on your clothing, bags, or hats for a fashionable accessory.

5. Felt bookmarks: Make personalized bookmarks using felt. Cut out a long rectangular shape from felt, and decorate it with buttons, sequins, or beads. You can also add decorative stitches or embroidery for an extra touch. Attach a tassel or a ribbon at one end to make it easy to find in your favorite book.

6. Felt coasters: Craft functional coasters for your home using felt. Cut out circular or square shapes from felt in various colors. Layer different colors together and secure them with fabric glue or stitching. These coasters not only protect your surfaces, but they also add a pop of color and style to your decor.

7. Felt garlands: Create whimsical garlands using felt shapes. Cut out different shapes, such as stars, hearts, or animals, from felt sheets. String them together using a needle and thread or twine. Hang the garland on walls, mantels, or windows to add a festive and playful touch to your space.

These are just a few examples of the many DIY felt crafts you can explore. Remember to let your creativity flow and experiment with different colors, shapes, and embellishments to make each project unique. With a little practice and patience, you will be amazed at the beautiful and artistic creations you can make with felt. Happy crafting!.

Chapter 10: Cork

- Introduction to Cork

Cork, derived from the bark of the cork oak tree, is a versatile and sustainable material that has gained popularity in various artistic and crafting endeavors.

Cork possesses unique properties that make it an excellent choice for a wide range of projects. It is lightweight, buoyant, insulating, and shock-absorbent, making it both practical and aesthetically pleasing. Its natural texture, warm tones, and earthy charm provide endless opportunities for experimentation and artistic expression.

Before delving into the world of cork crafting, it is important to familiarize yourself with the tools and materials you will need. Firstly, ensure that you have a good-quality cutting mat or board to protect your work surface and prolong the life of your cutting tools. Additionally, you will require a precision craft knife with a sharp blade, as cork can be thick and resistant to cutting. A metal ruler is indispensable for achieving straight and accurate cuts, while a self-healing rotary cutter is useful for more intricate or curved designs. Lastly, a fine-grit sandpaper will come in handy for smoothing rough edges and refining the finished product.

When working with cork, it is important to have a clear vision of your desired outcome. Sketch out your design or gather inspiration from various sources such as magazines, online platforms, or even your surroundings. Whether you are creating coasters, jewelry, decorative objects, or something entirely unique, having a well-defined plan will ensure a cohesive and captivating end result.

Once you have your design in mind, it is time to decide on the type and thickness of cork that best suits your project. Cork sheets are commonly available in various sizes, ranging from thin sheets suitable for delicate crafts to thicker ones ideal for more robust creations. Take into consideration the final purpose of your piece and the level of intricacy your design requires.

Some projects may benefit from the natural cork's thickness, while others will necessitate the use of thinner options.

When it comes to adhering cork to different surfaces or joining various cork pieces together, selecting the appropriate adhesive is paramount. There are multiple options available, including craft glue, hot glue, double-sided adhesive sheets, and even cork-specific adhesives. Experimentation will help you determine which adhesive suits your project best, ensuring a secure and long-lasting bond.

One of the most exciting aspects of working with cork is the ability to personalize and embellish your creations. Consider incorporating other materials such as fabric, lace, or even metal accents to add depth and visual interest to your project. Cork can be easily combined with various decorative elements, enabling you to explore an array of textures, patterns, and colors that will truly enhance your DIY endeavor.

As you progress in your cork crafting journey, don't be afraid to experiment and push the boundaries of your creativity. Try incorporating different techniques such as stamping, painting, or burning to achieve unique effects and textures. Embrace imperfections and understand that they contribute to the individuality and charm of your handmade item.

With the right tools, clear vision, and a willingness to experiment, you can unleash your creativity and produce outstanding cork-based crafts. From coasters to jewelry, decor pieces to unique gifts, cork will undoubtedly elevate your artistic endeavors like never before. Embrace the world of cork as you embark on an exciting journey of discovery and craftsmanship.

- Different Types of Cork

Cork is a versatile material that can be used in a variety of DIY projects. Its unique texture and natural look make it ideal for adding interest and dimension to your crafts.

There are several types of cork available on the market, each with its own characteristics and uses. Natural cork is the most common type and is harvested from the bark of the cork oak tree. It is light in color and has a soft, spongy texture. Natural cork is easy to work with and is suitable for a wide range of crafts.

Another type of cork that you may come across is colored cork. This cork has been dyed during the manufacturing process and is available in a variety of vibrant hues. Colored cork can add a pop of color to your projects and can be especially useful for creating eye-catching decorations.

For those looking for a more unique and rustic look, there is also textured cork. This type of cork has a rougher surface that adds a tactile element to your crafts. Textured cork can be great for adding interest to jewelry, home decor items, and even scrapbooking projects.

If you want to take your cork crafts to the next level, you may also want to consider cork sheets. These are larger pieces of cork that can be used for a multitude of purposes. You can cut them into shapes, use them as a base for other materials, or even cover entire surfaces with cork sheets.

In addition to the types of cork, you also have different thicknesses to choose from. Thin cork is great for adding small accents to your crafts, while thicker cork can be used for more substantial pieces. The thickness of the cork will depend on your project and personal preference, so make sure to experiment and find what works best for you.

When working with cork, it's important to have the right tools and materials. A sharp craft knife or scissors will be essential for cutting the cork to the desired shape and size. You may also need glue or adhesive to secure the cork to your project, depending on your design.

Whether you're embellishing a photo frame, creating unique jewelry, or adding texture to a scrapbook page, cork is a versatile and exciting material to work with. So, gather your supplies and let your creativity flow as you explore the possibilities of crafting with cork!.

- Cork Crafts Ideas

Cork, the versatile material derived from the bark of the cork oak tree, has gained popularity in the world of DIY crafting. Its unique texture and lightweight nature make it an ideal material for creating various crafts. In this chapter, we will explore some exciting DIY cork craft ideas that will inspire and spark your creativity.

1. Cork Coasters: Cork coasters are not only functional but also add a touch of elegance to your home décor. To create your cork coasters, you will need a collection of cork discs. These discs can either be purchased or can be cut from a corkboard sheet. Once you have your cork discs, you can paint them, decorate them with washi tape, or embellish them with sequins, beads, or even rhinestones. Let your imagination run wild!.

2. Cork Bulletin Board: Do you constantly find yourself searching for a place to pin important reminders, photos, or notes? Why not create your own cork bulletin board using cork tiles? Cork tiles can be easily found at any craft store. All you need to do is arrange them on a wooden frame or directly on a wall, securing them with glue or small nails. Once you have your bulletin board in place, you can decorate it further by adding colorful buttons, gemstones, charms, or even little pom-poms.

3. Cork Planters: Transform your old wine corks into adorable mini planters for succulents or small tabletop plants. Start by hollowing out the center of each cork using a small drill or knife, ensuring you don't damage the outer layer of the cork. Add a layer of soil, and insert a small succulent or plant of your choice. These tiny cork planters can be used as cute decorations as well as unique party favors or gifts.

4. Cork Jewelry: Create one-of-a-kind jewelry pieces using cork sheets. Cut out various shapes, such as circles, squares, or diamonds, from the cork sheet. You can paint them, cover them in fabric or felt, or adhere different materials like gemstones, sequins, or beads onto them. Once decorated, attach a jump

ring and a chain to transform the cork shapes into necklaces, bracelets, or even earrings.

5. Cork Keychains: For a personalized touch to your keys, make stylish cork keychains. Cut thin slices from a cork sheet and decorate them with glitter glue, sequins, or even small charms. Punch a hole at the top of the cork slice and attach a metal keychain ring. These unique keychains will not only help you find your keys but also add a creative flair to your daily routine.

There you have it – five exciting DIY cork craft ideas to get your creative juices flowing. Remember, the possibilities with cork crafts are endless. Experiment with different techniques, materials, and embellishments to create your own unique designs. Have fun exploring the world of cork crafts and let your artistic skills shine!.

Chapter 11: Washi tape

- Introduction to Washi tape

Washi tape, a popular crafting material, is a decorative adhesive tape that originates from Japan. It is made using traditional Japanese paper called washi, which is handcrafted from renewable materials like fibers from bamboo, rice, wheat, or hemp. This unique tape is known for its colorful and intricate designs, adding a touch of creativity to any DIY project. In this chapter, we will explore the various aspects of working with washi tape and the endless possibilities it offers.

Washi tape can be used in a multitude of paper crafts, and its applications are only limited by your imagination. Whether you're a seasoned crafter or just starting out, incorporating washi tape into your creations can instantly elevate their appearance. From scrapbooking and card making to decorating home accessories and personalizing gifts, washi tape adds a playful and stylish element to any project.

To begin using washi tape, gather your selection of tapes in various colors and patterns. The beauty of washi tape lies in its versatility, as it can easily be adhered, repositioned, and removed without damaging the surface beneath. This makes it perfect for those who value flexibility and creativity in their work.
.

When using washi tape, it is essential to ensure that the surface you will be applying it to is clean and dry. This will guarantee a strong and long-lasting bond. Start by tearing or cutting the desired length of tape, carefully applying it to your project. The edges can be neatly trimmed or torn for a more rustic and handmade look. .

One of the significant benefits of washi tape is that it can be layered or combined with other craft materials for added visual interest. Experiment with incorporating buttons, sequins, beads, rhinestones, gemstones, charms, pom-poms, feathers, felt, cork, and fabric into your washi tape projects. Not only will this create a unique and personalized aesthetic, but it will also showcase your creativity and skill as an artisan.

In addition to combining washi tape with other craft materials, it can also be used to create patterns, borders, and shapes. The versatility of this tape makes it an excellent choice for adding intricate detail to your paper crafts. It can also be used for creating backgrounds, frames, or highlighting specific elements in your designs. Let your imagination run wild and explore the countless possibilities of working with this wonderful tape.

When you have completed your project, take a moment to admire the beauty and charm that washi tape has added. Share your creations with friends, family, or fellow crafters to inspire and encourage others to explore the world of washi tape. The joy and satisfaction that comes from creating something unique and beautiful with your own hands are truly incomparable.

Its intricate designs, easy application, and ability to work seamlessly with other materials make it a favorite among artisans. Whether you are a beginner or an experienced crafter, incorporating washi tape into your projects will undoubtedly enhance their appearance and inject an element of creativity. So dive into the world of washi tape and let your artistic prowess shine through!.

- Different Types of Washi tape

Washi tape is a versatile and decorative adhesive tape that originated in Japan. It is made from natural fibers such as bamboo or hemp, which give it its unique texture and appearance. Washi tape comes in various colors, patterns, and widths, making it a perfect choice for adding a personal touch to your crafts.

When it comes to DIY paper crafts, Washi tape can be used in numerous ways. Let's explore some ideas and techniques for using Washi tape effectively with buttons, sequins, beads, rhinestones, gemstones, charms, pom-poms, feathers, felt, cork, fabric tape, duct tape, masking tape, glitter, glitter glue, sequin waste, tinsel, foil, and even aluminum foil.

Washi tape can be used as a delightful border or frame for your paper crafts featuring buttons. Simply adhere the tape around the edges of your project, and you'll instantly add a charming and colorful touch. Alternatively, you can create a button-themed design by layering different colors and patterns of Washi tape and attaching buttons on top.

For sequins, Washi tape provides an excellent base to stick them onto without the need for adhesive. Cut a small piece of Washi tape and apply it to your project. Choose sequins in various shapes and colors and attach them directly to the tape. You can create beautiful patterns and designs effortlessly.

Likewise, Washi tape serves as a reliable adhesive for beads, rhinestones, and gemstones. The tape's slightly textured surface allows for easy attachment of these embellishments. Whether you create intricate patterns or simply accentuate your design, Washi tape will keep your beads, rhinestones, and gemstones securely in place.

When it comes to attaching charms, pom-poms, feathers, or felt to your paper crafts, Washi tape can be your best friend. Its adhesive properties will ensure that your chosen embellishments stay firmly in place while adding a touch of creativity to your projects. Experiment with different combinations of Washi tape and materials to achieve unique and eye-catching results.

While Washi tape is traditionally used with paper crafts, it can also be paired with other materials such as cork, fabric tape, duct tape, masking tape, glitter, glitter glue, sequin waste, tinsel, foil, and aluminum foil. These materials can be easily adhered to your projects by using Washi tape as a bonding agent. The possibilities are endless, allowing you to explore new realms of creativity and design.

To create your DIY Washi tape, you will need a few basic supplies. Start with a roll of plain adhesive tape that has a width suitable for your intended project. Then, select your desired patterned tissue paper or decorative napkin. Cut the paper or napkin into pieces that match the length of your adhesive tape. Finally, adhere the paper or napkin onto the tape, using a craft stick or your fingers to smooth out any air bubbles or wrinkles.

By combining it with buttons, sequins, beads, rhinestones, gemstones, charms, pom-poms, feathers, felt, cork, fabric tape, duct tape, masking tape, glitter, glitter glue, sequin waste, tinsel, foil, and aluminum foil, you can create stunning and unique projects that showcase your personal style and creativity. Have fun experimenting with different combinations and let your imagination run wild with the endless possibilities that Washi tape offers!.

- Washi tape Crafts Ideas

Washi tape is a versatile material that is perfect for adding texture, color, and pattern to your DIY projects. It can be used in countless ways, whether you're creating home decor items, accessories, or gifts for loved ones. So, let's delve into some creative ideas using Washi tape!.

One of the easiest and most popular ways to use Washi tape is in DIY paper crafts. With just a few basic supplies like buttons, sequins, beads, rhinestones, gemstones, charms, pom-poms, feathers, or felt, along with Washi tape, you can create stunning and unique designs. When working with buttons, simply cut small strips of Washi tape and wrap them around the button's edges to create a fun and vibrant look. Or, layer different Washi tape patterns on top of each other to give the button a textured and multidimensional appearance.

Sequins are another fantastic embellishment that can be easily transformed with Washi tape. Start by applying the Washi tape on a piece of paper or cardstock and then use a sequin punch to cut out sequins. The sequins will have a beautiful Washi tape pattern on them, making them stand out in your projects. You can create a dramatic effect by mixing different colors and patterns of Washi tape or pair sequins with matching Washi tape to create a cohesive look.

Beads are a classic embellishment that adds a touch of elegance to any project. With Washi tape, you can create your unique beads that reflect your personal style. Cut long strips of Washi tape and wrap them tightly around a toothpick or skewer until you have a tube-like shape. Slide the newly formed Washi tape beads off the toothpick and use a piece of string or wire to create various jewelry pieces. By using different patterns and colors of Washi tape, you can craft stunning and one-of-a-kind accessories.

Rhinestones and gemstones are fantastic for adding a touch of sparkle to your projects. You can enhance their beauty even further by incorporating Washi tape. Cut small squares of Washi tape and apply them to the back of your rhinestones or gemstones. Trimming the edges will give your embellishments a polished look. These Washi tape backing enhances their appearance when you use adhesive to attach them to your desired craft project.

Charms are delicate and beautiful additions to any DIY project. With Washi tape, you can easily personalize your charms by adding textures and patterns. Cut small pieces of Washi tape, apply one side of the tape to the charm, and fold the excess over to the back. You can layer different patterns or colors of Washi tape and trim any excess with a craft knife or scissors. Your newly decorated charm will have a unique and eye-catching design.

Pom-poms are fun and whimsical embellishments that can be transformed with Washi tape. For a playful look, wrap strands of Washi tape around the pom-pom, leaving some gaps in between for the fluffy texture to peek through. You can also experiment with different patterns and color combinations to create custom-made pom-poms that perfectly suit your style or theme.

Feathers are delicate and versatile additions to any craft project. With Washi tape, you can take them to new heights. Simply cut small pieces of Washi tape and apply them to the base of the feather. You can create ombre effects, stripes, or geometric patterns by layering different tapes together or use complementary colors for an elegant and sophisticated look.

Felt is an excellent material for creating soft and durable embellishments. Pair it with Washi tape to add depth and visual interest to your designs. To create a Washi tape-infused felt embellishment, start by cutting out your desired shape from the felt. Then, cut small strips or pieces of Washi tape and adhere them to the felt. You can create eye-catching patterns, stripes, or entirely cover the felt piece with Washi tape for a unique and artistic touch.

Cork is a material that blends well with Washi tape, giving your crafts a natural and rustic appearance. You can wrap strips of Washi tape around cork coasters, create custom cork boards by covering them entirely with Washi tape, or cut out shapes from cork sheets and decorate them with Washi tape accents. The possibilities are endless, and you'll end up with charming and stylish home decor pieces.

By incorporating Washi tape into your DIY projects, you can add color, pattern, and texture to your designs. Whether you're working with buttons, sequins, beads, rhinestones, gemstones, charms, pom-poms, feathers, felt, cork, or any other material mentioned in this book, Washi tape offers endless possibilities for creative expression. Embrace your inner artisan and let your imagination run wild with Washi tape!.

Chapter 12: Fabric tape

- Introduction to Fabric tape

Fabric tape is a versatile and popular crafting material that can add a touch of elegance and creativity to your DIY projects. Made from fabric with adhesive backing, fabric tape allows you to easily embellish and decorate various surfaces with ease.

When it comes to DIY Paper Crafts, fabric tape can be a valuable tool for adding texture and visual interest to your creations. Whether you are working with buttons, sequins, beads, rhinestones, gemstones, charms, pom-poms, feathers, felt, cork, washi tape, duct tape, masking tape, glitter, glitter glue, sequin waste, tinsel, foil, or even aluminum foil, fabric tape can complement these materials beautifully.

For many crafters, fabric tape is especially popular due to its ease of use. With its adhesive backing, it can be easily applied to different surfaces, including paper. To use fabric tape in your paper crafts, simply cut a desired length of the tape and remove the backing, revealing the adhesive side. Press the tape onto your project, making sure to smooth out any wrinkles or air bubbles for a clean finish. The strong adhesive ensures that the fabric tape stays in place, even on curved or irregular surfaces.

One of the great things about fabric tape is that it comes in a wide range of colors, patterns, and textures. This allows you to find the perfect tape to match your project, whether you are aiming for a sophisticated, whimsical, or bold look. Explore different options and experiment with layering different tapes to create unique designs and effects.

Fabric tape is not limited to paper crafts, and its uses extend to various other DIY projects. It can be applied to fabrics and clothing to add decorative accents or repair small tears or holes. You can also use fabric tape to create fabric-based crafts such as bows, rosettes, and flowers. It can be easily cut into different shapes and sizes, giving you the freedom to unleash your creativity.

Aside from its aesthetic qualities, fabric tape also offers practical benefits. Its adhesive backing is usually durable and long-lasting, ensuring that your creations remain intact for a significant amount of time. Fabric tape is also often machine washable, making it ideal for clothing or fabric-based projects that require regular cleaning.

When working with fabric tape, it is important to handle it carefully and store it in a cool, dry place to maintain its adhesive qualities. If you are working on a project that requires precise alignment or a specific pattern, it can be helpful to use a ruler or a template to guide your application. Take your time and ensure that the tape is applied neatly and smoothly for the best results.

Its ease of use, versatility, and wide range of colors and patterns make it a valuable material for embellishing and enhancing various projects, from paper crafts to fabric-based creations. So why not give fabric tape a try and bring your crafting endeavors to a whole new level? Happy crafting!.

- Types of Fabric tape

Fabric tape is a versatile decorative material that can be easily customized to suit your creative needs. It can be made from a wide range of fabrics, such as cotton, silk, satin, or even lace. The possibilities are endless! Let's delve into the details of each type of fabric tape and explore the techniques to create them.

Cotton fabric tape is a popular choice due to its wide availability and durability. To make cotton fabric tape, start by selecting a fabric with a design or color that complements your project. Cut the fabric into thin strips, about 1-2 inches wide. If you prefer a frayed look, leave the edges unfinished. To prevent fraying, fold the edges inward and secure with fabric glue or by stitching. You can also decorate the fabric by adding embroidery, fabric paint, or heat transfer designs. The resulting cotton fabric tape will be a stylish addition to any craft project.

Satin fabric tape adds a touch of elegance to your creations. To create satin fabric tape, choose a satin fabric in the desired color. Cut the fabric into strips of the same width as the cotton fabric tape. Satin tends to fray easily, so it is essential to finish the edges. You can achieve this by folding the edges inward and securing them with fabric glue or stitching. Satin fabric tape works beautifully in jewelry making, clothing embellishments, or as a decorative border on cards and invitations.

For those looking for a glamorous option, lace fabric tape is the perfect choice. Lace adds a delicate and intricate detail to any project. To make lace fabric tape, select a lace trim that matches the width of the previously mentioned fabric tapes. Cut the lace into strips of the desired length. Just like satin, lace also tends to fray. To prevent this, apply fabric glue to the edges or use a sewing machine to stitch along the edges. Lace fabric tape can be used to adorn scrapbooks, gift wrapping, or even as an elegant trim on clothing and accessories.

Now that you have learned how to create fabric tape, let's explore some creative ideas for using it in your DIY paper crafts. Fabric tape can be used to embellish buttons, sequins, beads, rhinestones, gemstones, charms, pom-poms, feathers, felt, cork, washi tape, and even duct tape. Simply cut small pieces of fabric tape and apply them to these materials to add a unique and textured look.

Additionally, fabric tape can be used as a background for glitter, glitter glue, sequin waste, tinsel, foil, and aluminum foil. Apply a strip of fabric tape onto your project and sprinkle or adhere these materials onto it for a stunning effect. The fabric tape acts as a base that holds the embellishments securely in place.

By creating your own fabric tape using cotton, satin, or lace, you have the flexibility to customize it to your needs. Use fabric tape to embellish various materials and experiment with combining it with different embellishments for a unique and eye-catching result. With these techniques, your DIY paper crafts will have an added touch of style and creativity.

- Fabric tape Crafts Ideas

In this chapter, we will explore a variety of creative and innovative DIY projects utilizing fabric tape. Fabric tape, also known as fabric washi tape, is a versatile and fun material to work with. It comes in a wide range of colors, patterns, and sizes, allowing you to customize your creations to suit your personal taste and style. Whether you are a seasoned DIY enthusiast or just starting out, fabric tape crafts offer endless possibilities for expressing your creativity.

Fabric tape is made of fabric material with an adhesive backing, similar to regular washi tape. This adhesive backing makes it easy to stick the tape onto various surfaces, including paper, cardboard, fabric, and even glass. The tape is also repositionable, meaning you can remove it and stick it again without leaving any residue. This feature is particularly useful when working on intricate designs or when you want to make adjustments to your project.

One of the simplest and most enjoyable fabric tape crafts is creating decorative gift wrapping. Instead of using plain paper and conventional ribbons, you can add a pop of color and pattern by using fabric tape. Start by selecting a roll of fabric tape that complements your gift's theme or the recipient's preferences. You can opt for festive patterns for holidays, floral designs for birthdays, or pastel hues for baby showers.

To begin, wrap the gift with plain or colored paper and secure it with regular tape. Then, select the desired fabric tape and cut off a piece that is slightly longer than the width of the gift. Place the tape horizontally or vertically across the wrapped gift, alternating directions or creating a specific pattern. Smooth out any wrinkles or air bubbles in the tape, ensuring a sleek and polished appearance. Finally, trim any excess tape, if necessary, and you have a beautifully wrapped gift that is sure to impress.

Another creative application of fabric tape is in the realm of home decor. You can transform ordinary household items into unique and eye-catching pieces with just a little fabric tape. Let's take a look at a few examples to inspire your own DIY projects.

- Picture Frames: Give your old picture frames a fresh and modern look by covering the outer edges with fabric tape. Choose a tape that complements the colors in the photo or the overall color scheme of the room. Simply measure and cut the tape to fit the frame and press it firmly onto the surface. Smooth out any bubbles or wrinkles, and you have a customized frame that adds a pop of color to your cherished memories.

- Flower Pots: Add a touch of whimsy to your indoor or outdoor plants by decorating their pots with fabric tape. Whether you prefer solid colors or vibrant patterns, fabric tape can instantly elevate the appearance of plain terracotta pots. Start by thoroughly cleaning the pot and allowing it to dry completely. Then, measure and cut the fabric tape to fit around the pot, pressing it firmly onto the surface. Repeat this process for all sides of the pot until it is completely covered. The result is a fun and personalized decoration that will bring joy to any space.

- Lamp Shades: Give your lamps a makeover by embellishing their shades with fabric tape. This is a fantastic way to update outdated or plain lamp shades without spending a fortune. Choose a fabric tape that complements the overall design aesthetic of the room. Start by measuring the length of the shade and cut the tape accordingly. Position the tape vertically, horizontally, or diagonally on the shade, creating a pattern or design that suits your preference. Smooth out any imperfections or air bubbles, and your lamp will be instantly transformed into an artful piece of functional decor.

These are just a few ideas to get you started on your fabric tape crafts journey. With the endless variety of fabric tape colors, patterns, and sizes available, your imagination is the only limit in creating unique and personalized projects. So, gather your materials, let your creativity flow, and have fun experimenting with fabric tape in your DIY endeavors!.

Chapter 13: Duct tape

- Introduction to Duct tape

Duct tape is a versatile and practical material that has gained immense popularity in the DIY community. Its adhesive properties and durability make it a go-to product for a wide range of crafting projects. Whether you are a beginner or an experienced artisan, understanding the potential of duct tape can open doors to countless creative possibilities.

To begin your journey with duct tape, it is important to understand its properties and characteristics. Duct tape is a strong adhesive tape that is made from cloth backed with a polyethylene coating. This combination gives it strength and flexibility, making it suitable for a variety of applications. Additionally, duct tape is available in a vast array of colors and patterns, allowing you to personalize your creations even further.

When working with duct tape, it is crucial to have the right tools and supplies. To start, gather a pair of scissors, a cutting mat, a ruler or tape measure, and, of course, a collection of duct tape. These basic tools will empower you to explore the limitless potential of duct tape.

Before diving into specific projects, it is essential to familiarize yourself with some foundational techniques. Firstly, the tearing technique is a simple yet effective way to cut duct tape. Rather than using scissors, tear the tape by folding it over and pulling it apart. This technique will create clean edges and is ideal for quick and easy cuts.

Another technique is called layering, which involves overlapping multiple strips of duct tape to create unique designs and color combinations. Layering can add depth and texture to your creations, transforming ordinary objects into eye-catching works of art.

Furthermore, duct tape can also be used to create patterns and textures through techniques like braiding, weaving, and pleating. These techniques offer endless opportunities for adding intricate detailing to your projects.

Now that you have learned the basics, let's explore some DIY paper crafts using duct tape. One popular idea is to create buttons using duct tape. To do this, start by cutting a strip of duct tape and folding it in half, sticky sides facing each other. Then, punch out circles or use a round template to cut out button shapes. Remove the backing and adhere the button to your project or attach a sewing button to the back for added functionality.

Another paper craft idea using duct tape is to create sequins. Cut small rectangles of duct tape and fold them in half lengthwise, sticky sides facing each other. Next, trim the folded tape into triangle shapes, resembling sequins. These duct tape sequins can be glued onto greeting cards, scrapbook pages, or other paper crafts to add a touch of sparkle and dimension.

In addition to buttons and sequins, you can also experiment with creating beads, rhinestones, gemstones, charms, pom-poms, feathers, and more using duct tape. Let your imagination roam free and explore the vast possibilities that duct tape offers.

Its adhesive strength, variety of patterns, and ease of use make it a top-choice for DIY enthusiasts. By familiarizing yourself with duct tape's properties and mastering some basic techniques, you can utilize this versatile material to enhance your projects and unleash your creativity. Whether you are embellishing paper crafts, decorating home décor items, or venturing into wearable art, duct tape is a fantastic addition to your crafting toolbox. So go ahead, grab some duct tape, and let your imagination run wild!.

- Different Types of Duct tape

In this chapter, we will explore the fascinating world of Duct tape and its various types. Duct tape is a versatile material that can be used in numerous DIY projects. Its strong adhesive properties and durability make it an excellent choice for various crafting needs.

Duct tape comes in a wide range of styles, colors, and patterns, allowing you to get as creative as you want with your projects.

1. Washi Tape: Also known as decorative tape, Washi tape is a type of Duct tape made from natural fibers such as bamboo or hemp. It features delicate patterns and vibrant colors, making it perfect for adding a touch of elegance and style to any craft project.

2. Fabric Tape: This type of Duct tape is made from fabric materials, giving it a softer and more textured feel compared to traditional Duct tape. The fabric tape can be easily torn by hand, making it convenient to work with. It is often used for fabric-related crafts, including sewing projects and garment repairs.

3. Masking Tape: Although not specifically designed as a Duct tape, masking tape can still be a useful alternative. It is a light adhesive tape that is easy to tear and remove without leaving behind any residue. Masking tape is commonly used in painting projects to create clean edges and protect surfaces.

4. Glitter: If you want to add some sparkle and glam to your project, glitter Duct tape is the way to go. It is a fun and eye-catching type of Duct tape that is covered in tiny shimmering particles. Glitter Duct tape is perfect for creating dazzling accessories or adding a touch of festivity to party decorations.

5. Glitter Glue: While not exactly a type of Duct tape, glitter glue is worth mentioning due to its ability to enhance your Duct tape crafts. It comes in various colors and can be used to create intricate designs or add a shiny finish to your projects.

6. Sequin Waste: Also known as sequin trim, sequin waste is a strip of fabric or plastic adorned with small sequins. You can find sequin waste in various

colors, sizes, and shapes, allowing you to add a touch of glamour to your Duct tape crafts.

7. Tinsel: If you're feeling festive, tinsel Duct tape can help you create projects with a merry and bright vibe. This type of Duct tape features metallic strands woven into the adhesive, giving it a shimmering and celebratory appearance.

8. Foil: Foil Duct tape is a unique type of Duct tape that comes in metallic colors, giving your projects a sleek and futuristic touch. It works well for creating crafts with a modern aesthetic or for adding reflective surfaces to your designs.

9. Aluminum foil: Another unconventional yet interesting option is using regular aluminum foil as a Duct tape substitute. While not specifically designed for crafting purposes, aluminum foil can be manipulated to create a variety of textures and effects.

Each type of Duct tape mentioned above offers a unique set of characteristics, allowing you to choose the right one for your project. Whether you're looking to add sparkle, elegance, or a festive touch, there's a Duct tape out there that will fit your needs. Stay crafty!.

- Duct tape Crafts Ideas

Duct tape is a versatile material that can be used to make a wide range of crafts and accessories. From wallets and bags to flowers and jewelry, the possibilities are endless. So, let's get started and see how we can unleash our creativity with duct tape!.

Duct Tape Wallet:

One popular and simple duct tape project is a wallet. To make a duct tape wallet, you will need a roll of colored duct tape, a pair of scissors, and a ruler. Start by cutting two rectangular pieces of duct tape, each measuring 8 inches by 3 inches. Stick the two pieces together, leaving a small gap at the top for a card slot. Fold the piece in half, leaving one side slightly longer to act as a flap. Trim any excess tape and secure the edges by folding over thin strips of tape. Your duct tape wallet is now ready to be used!.

Duct Tape Flowers:

Another fun and creative duct tape craft idea is making duct tape flowers. For this project, gather some colored duct tapes, scissors, and a pipe cleaner. Start by cutting a strip of duct tape, about 6 inches long. Fold the strip in half, sticky side inwards, and fold it in half again. Now, cut small strips along the fold, making sure not to cut all the way through. Unfold the strip and roll it up tightly to form a flower shape. Finally, attach a pipe cleaner to the bottom of the flower to create a stem. You can make several flowers and arrange them in a bouquet or use them to decorate gift wraps and cards.

Duct Tape Jewelry:

With duct tape, you can also create unique and stylish jewelry pieces. To make a duct tape bracelet, cut a strip of duct tape, about 2 inches wide and long enough to fit around your wrist. Fold the strip in half, sticky side inwards, and press firmly. Trim any excess tape and attach a snap button or Velcro at the ends to secure the bracelet. You can experiment with different colors and patterns to create a personalized collection of duct tape bracelets.

Duct Tape Bags:

If you're feeling adventurous, you can even make a duct tape bag. To create a duct tape bag, you will need a large piece of cardboard, colored duct tapes, scissors, and a rotary cutter. Start by cutting the cardboard into the desired shape and size of your bag. Cover the cardboard with strips of duct tape, leaving no cardboard exposed. Fold the edges neatly and secure them with additional strips of tape. Create straps for the bag by cutting two long pieces of duct tape, around 16 inches each, and attaching them to the sides of the bag. Your unique duct tape bag is now complete!.

You can make wallets, flowers, jewelry, bags and many more exciting projects using just duct tape. So gather your supplies, let your imagination run wild, and start creating incredible duct tape crafts today!.

Chapter 14: Masking tape

- Introduction to Masking tape

Masking tape is a versatile tool that can be used in a wide range of DIY projects. Whether you are a beginner or an experienced artisan, incorporating masking tape into your creative process can add a unique touch to your crafts. In this chapter, we will explore the various ways in which you can use masking tape to enhance your projects. .

Before we delve into the different techniques, it is important to understand what masking tape is and why it is commonly used in crafting. Masking tape is a type of adhesive tape that is made from a thin and easy-to-tear paper. It features a gentle adhesive that allows it to be easily removed without leaving any residue.

One of the key benefits of masking tape is its ability to temporarily hold materials together during the crafting process. It creates a secure bond, ensuring that your project stays intact while you work with other elements. Masking tape can also act as a guide or barrier, helping you create straight lines or prevent paint from bleeding onto certain areas.

In DIY paper crafts, masking tape can be a valuable tool. You can use it to create patterns or designs on paper, as it can be easily adhered and removed without damaging the surface. This makes it ideal for creating temporary stencils or masking off specific areas when applying color or texture.

For example, if you are working on a button-themed paper craft, you can use masking tape to outline the shape of the buttons on your paper before painting or coloring. This will help you achieve clean and precise lines. Masking tape can also be used to create interesting textures or backgrounds by layering it and painting over it.

When it comes to sequins, beads, rhinestones, gemstones, charms, pom-poms, feathers, felt, cork, washi tape, fabric tape, duct tape, and masking tape, there are numerous creative applications. For masking tape specifically, it can be used to secure the edges of sequins, beads, rhinestones, gemstones, and charms onto your craft projects. The tape provides a temporary hold, allowing you to experiment and reposition the embellishments until you are satisfied with the final arrangement.

Furthermore, masking tape can also be used to create interactive elements in your crafts. You can attach feathers or felt cutouts to a piece of masking tape and adhere it to your project, providing a tactile experience for the viewer. These elements can easily be removed or replaced as desired.

It is worth mentioning that masking tape is available in various widths and colors, making it even more versatile for your crafting needs. You can experiment with different thicknesses and hues to achieve different effects and enhance the overall aesthetic of your project.

To conclude, masking tape is a valuable tool in the DIY creative realm. Its gentle adhesive and easy removal make it ideal for temporary applications, such as stenciling, marking, or securing embellishments in place. Incorporating masking tape into your crafts can add a unique touch and open up endless possibilities for your creative expression. So go ahead and explore the world of masking tape and see how it can elevate your crafting endeavors.

- Types of Masking tape

Masking tape is an essential tool for crafters and artisans, as it offers a multitude of creative possibilities. From basic paper crafts to intricate embellishments, masking tape can be the perfect companion for your artistic endeavors.

This tape is made from a thin and flexible paper material, which allows for easy tearing and application. It is ideal for masking off areas when painting or creating intricate designs. With its adhesive properties, it firmly adheres to most surfaces and can be easily removed without leaving any residue or damaging the underlying material.

Another popular type of masking tape is the colored masking tape. Available in a wide range of vibrant hues, these tapes allow you to add a pop of color and visual interest to your crafts. Colored masking tape is particularly useful for creating decorative borders, patterns, and designs on various surfaces. Its adhesive properties are similar to the traditional beige masking tape, ensuring a secure hold while being easily removable.

For those who prefer a bit of extra flair in their crafts, there are also specialty masking tapes available. These include metallic masking tape, glitter masking tape, and patterned masking tape. Metallic masking tape adds a touch of elegance and shine to your projects, making it perfect for festive decorations or intricate jewelry designs. Glitter masking tape, as the name suggests, features a glimmering surface that adds a sparkly effect to your crafts. Patterned masking tape comes in a variety of designs, allowing you to create unique and eye-catching patterns on your crafts.

Washi tape is a type of masking tape that originates from Japan. It is made from traditional Japanese paper and comes in a vast array of patterns and colors. Washi tape is known for its decorative qualities and is commonly used in scrapbooking, card-making, and other paper crafts. Its adhesive properties are similar to traditional masking tape, making it easy to adhere and remove without causing damage.

Fabric tape is another variation of masking tape that is specifically designed for use on fabric materials. It has a cloth-like texture and is perfect for securing fabric edges, hemming, or adding decorative trim to your sewing projects. Fabric tape is often heat-activated, meaning that it can be affixed using an iron or by applying heat, ensuring a secure and permanent hold.

Duct tape, although not traditionally considered a masking tape, is a versatile option that can be used for a variety of purposes. It is known for its strong adhesive properties and durability, making it suitable for both practical and artistic uses. From repairing household items to creating sturdy crafts, duct tape is a reliable choice for any DIY enthusiast.

Masking tape, as a whole, is an indispensable tool for any crafter. Its versatility and ease of use make it a must-have for various projects. Whether you're a beginner or an experienced artisan, there is a masking tape type that will suit your creative needs. So go ahead, explore the amazing world of masking tape, and let your imagination run wild!.

- Masking tape Crafts Ideas

Masking tape, also known as painter's tape, is a versatile and adhesive craft supply that can be used creatively in various DIY projects. Let's dive in!.

One of the easiest and most popular crafts involving masking tape is DIY Paper Crafts. You can use masking tape to create unique and eye-catching designs on plain paper or cardstock. Simply tear off strips of masking tape and stick them onto the paper in desired patterns, angles, or shapes. You can experiment with different colors of masking tape to add vibrancy to your designs. Once you are satisfied with the arrangement, you can apply paint, ink, or any other coloring medium over the paper. When the paint is dry, carefully remove the masking tape to reveal the crisp and clean lines of the masked area. This technique allows you to create visually appealing backgrounds or focal points for your paper crafts.

Another fascinating idea is to incorporate buttons into your masking tape crafts. Start by selecting a button of your choice. Then, tear off a small strip of masking tape and stick it onto the button, making sure to cover the holes. You can then paint over the tape to match the color of the button or go for a contrasting look. This simple technique gives you the opportunity to customize your buttons and use them in a variety of craft projects, such as jewelry making, scrapbooking, or clothing embellishments.

Sequins are another delightful embellishment that can be combined with masking tape. Take a sheet of masking tape and cut out small shapes, such as circles or hearts. Peel off the backing and stick the sequencing firmly onto the adhesive side of the masking tape. You can create patterns or arrangements with the sequins to achieve different effects. Once you are done, carefully peel off the masking tape and transfer the sequins onto your desired surface, such as a card, canvas, or fabric. This technique allows you to easily apply sequins without the need for messy glue.

Beads are a classic and elegant addition to any craft project. To incorporate beads into your masking tape crafts, begin by tearing off a strip of masking tape and sticking it onto a clean surface. Then, place beads onto the sticky side of the tape, experimenting with different arrangements and patterns. Once you are happy with the design, carefully cut out the tape with beads into desired shapes or sizes. You can use these beaded masking tape pieces in various ways, such as jewelry making, home decor, or even as embellishments for greeting cards.

Rhinestones and gemstones can add a touch of sparkle and glamour to your masking tape crafts. Start by cutting a piece of masking tape in the desired size and shape. Then, peel off the backing and carefully place the rhinestones or gemstones onto the sticky side of the tape. You can arrange them in intricate patterns or create a simple design by placing them evenly apart. Once you are satisfied with the arrangement, peel off the masking tape and transfer the rhinestones or gemstones to your desired surface. These dazzling creations can be used to embellish phone cases, mirrors, picture frames, or any other surface you want to add a touch of bling to.

Charms are another fantastic addition to your masking tape crafts. Start by attaching the charm onto a piece of masking tape, making sure it is centered and secure. Then, use a craft blade to carefully cut around the charm, leaving a small border of masking tape around it. This technique not only creates a framed effect for the charm but also adds stability to the adhesive. You can then peel off the backing and attach the charm onto your desired surface. This technique works wonderfully for creating personalized charm jewelry or even adding charms to notebooks and journals.

Pom-poms, feathers, and felt can also be incorporated into your masking tape crafts. Begin by tearing off a strip of masking tape and sticking it onto a clean surface. Then, attach pom-poms, feathers, or pieces of felt onto the adhesive side of the tape, arranging them in desired patterns or shapes. Once you are satisfied with the design, carefully peel off the masking tape and transfer the decorated tape onto your desired surface. This technique allows you to create textured and dimensional designs, perfect for adding a playful and whimsical touch to your crafts.

Moving on to the various tapes in our list, let's start with washi tape. Washi tape is a decorative masking tape that comes in a wide variety of colors, patterns, and designs. It's perfect for adding a pop of color and pattern to your masking tape crafts. You can tear off strips of washi tape and stick them onto any surface to create interesting backgrounds, borders, or accents. You can also use washi tape as a masking technique itself by placing it onto an area you want to protect while working on another part of your craft. Once your project is complete, simply peel off the tape to reveal the clean lines and protected areas.

Fabric tape, like washi tape, is another type of decorative masking tape that can be used in various crafting projects. Its fabric-like texture adds a unique and tactile element to your creations. You can tear off strips of fabric tape and use them to cover surfaces, wrap objects, or create patterns. Fabric tape is particularly advantageous for fabric-based projects, such as clothing embellishments or textile art, as it easily adheres to fabric without causing damage or leaving residue.

Duct tape is a durable and strong adhesive tape that is commonly used in repair projects. However, it can also be creatively utilized in masking tape crafts. Duct tape comes in various colors and patterns, making it a versatile and fun material to work with. You can tear off strips of duct tape and use them to create DIY wallets, flower pots, or even costumes. You can also combine duct tape with other craft supplies, such as buttons or sequins, to create unique and customized designs.

Last but certainly not least, we have the star of this chapter - masking tape. Masking tape, as mentioned earlier, is a versatile and adhesive craft supply that can be used creatively in various DIY projects. Its ability to stick and remove easily without leaving residue makes it perfect for masking and protecting areas during painting or other craft processes. You can tear off strips of masking tape and create intriguing geometric designs, use it to secure stencils or templates, or apply it as a temporary guide for your painting or drawing. The possibilities are endless with masking tape, so feel free to experiment and see where your creativity takes you.

So don't be afraid to let your imagination run wild and try new techniques or combinations. Happy crafting!.

Chapter 15: Glitter

- Introduction to Glitter

Glitter, a dazzling material that instantly adds sparkle and glamour to any project, has become a popular choice among crafters, artists, and DIY enthusiasts. If you are looking to enhance your creations with an extra touch of pizzazz, incorporating glitter into your designs can be a game-changer. In this chapter, we will delve into the world of glitter and explore its various applications and techniques that can take your DIY endeavors to the next level.

Glitter provides a vibrant and eye-catching effect that can transform ordinary objects into extraordinary ones. Whether you are working with paper, fabric, or other materials, adding glitter can create a stunning visual impact. It opens up endless possibilities for customization and personalization, allowing you to breathe life into your creations and make them truly unique.

One of the first things you need to consider when working with glitter is the type of glitter you want to use. There are various types available in the market, such as fine glitter, chunky glitter, holographic glitter, and iridescent glitter. Each type offers a different texture, shine, and reflective quality, allowing you to choose the one that best suits your design vision.

Before applying glitter, it is essential to prepare your surface properly. For paper crafts, make sure the paper is clean and free from any dust or dirt particles. This will ensure that the glitter adheres to the surface uniformly and creates a smooth and even finish. Similarly, if you are working on fabrics, pre-wash and dry them to remove any chemicals or residues that might hinder the glitter's adhesion.

Once your surface is prepared, you can start applying the glitter. Begin by applying a thin, even layer of glue or adhesive on the desired area. You can use specialized glitter glue or opt for a clear-drying adhesive, such as white glue, which works just as effectively. It is important to work in small sections as glitter tends to dry quickly, and you want to ensure the adhesive remains tacky when applying the glitter.

To apply the glitter, simply sprinkle it over the adhesive-covered area. You can do this by gently tapping the glitter container or using a brush to distribute it evenly. Make sure to cover the entire adhesive area, leaving no gaps or patches. Once applied, gently press down on the glitter to ensure it properly adheres to the surface. Let it dry completely before removing any excess glitter.

To remove excess glitter, you can use a soft brush or a lint-free cloth to gently brush away the loose particles. If you find any areas with sparse glitter, you can reapply adhesive and add more glitter until you achieve the desired effect. Remember to handle the glitter with care to avoid unnecessary spillage or wastage.

Glitter can be used in numerous DIY projects, such as greeting cards, gift wrapping, party decorations, scrapbooking, and more. Its versatility allows you to explore various techniques, such as creating glitter gradients, mixing different glitter colors, or combining glitter with other embellishments like sequins, beads, or rhinestones for a multidimensional effect.

Moreover, glitter is not limited to just crafts; it can also be used in home decor projects, fashion accessories, and even for temporary embellishments like glitter tattoos or nail art. The possibilities truly are endless when it comes to utilizing glitter in your DIY endeavors.

Its shimmering brilliance and ability to catch the light will turn ordinary creations into extraordinary ones. With careful preparation, proper application, and an artistic eye, you can create stunning and captivating designs that will leave a lasting impression. So go ahead and explore the magical world of glitter, and let your creativity shine!.

- Different Types of Glitter

Glitter is a truly magical element that brings sparkle and allure to any craft project. With its shimmering particles catching the light, it adds a touch of glamour and delight to DIY creations.

Loose Glitter:

Loose glitter is perhaps the most common and versatile type of glitter. It comes in a powdered form, allowing for easy application and a seamless blend into your artwork. This type of glitter typically comes in a variety of colors and sizes, enabling you to create different effects and textures. For a stronger bond, you can mix loose glitter with glue or a glaze medium before applying it to your project.

Glitter Glue:

Glitter glue, as the name suggests, is a combination of glue and glitter particles. This type of glitter eliminates the need for separate adhesive and glitter, offering convenience and ease of use. Glitter glue is available in tubes or bottles, and you can apply it directly onto your craft piece. It is particularly useful for creating precise and controlled designs, as it dries quickly and adheres firmly.

Sequin Waste:

Sequin waste, also known as sequin confetti, is a unique form of glitter. It is composed of small, irregularly shaped sequins that create a mesmerizing shimmer. Sequin waste is usually supplied in small bags or containers and can be applied onto your project using glue or double-sided tape. It is an excellent choice for adding texture and dimension to your crafts, as well as creating eye-catching backgrounds or accents.

Tinsel:

Tinsel glitter is a type of glitter made from thin, metallic strips. It mimics the appearance of traditional holiday tinsel, adding a festive touch to your creations. Tinsel glitter is available in various colors, and its reflective properties make it ideal for capturing attention and creating a captivating visual impact.

You can apply tinsel glitter using glue or by mixing it with other mediums to create unique effects.

Foil:

Foil glitter, similar to tinsel glitter, consists of thin, metallic sheets that are stunningly reflective. It comes in a range of colors, including metallic shades, and can be cut into different shapes and sizes to suit your needs. Foil glitter adds a luxurious and glamorous touch to your crafts, and you can adhere it to your project using glue or by applying heat with a laminating machine or a heat tool.

Aluminum Foil:

Aluminum foil is a distinctive option for glitter enthusiasts seeking an unconventional touch. Rather than purchasing glitter, you can create your own by tearing small pieces of aluminum foil and adhering them to your project using craft glue or tape. Aluminum foil provides a unique texture and shine, which can transform ordinary crafts into extraordinary works of art.

By identifying and utilizing the many types of glitter available, you can effortlessly add sparkle and glamour to your DIY paper crafts. Whether you opt for loose glitter, glitter glue, sequin waste, tinsel, foil, or aluminum foil, each type offers its own unique properties and effects. So, embrace your creativity and experiment with different glitter options to achieve stunning and dazzling creations.

- Glitter Crafts Ideas

In this chapter, we will explore various techniques and ideas for incorporating glitter into your crafts. Glitter can be used with a wide range of materials, including paper, buttons, sequins, beads, rhinestones, gemstones, charms, pom-poms, feathers, felt, cork, washi tape, fabric tape, duct tape, masking tape, sequin waste, tinsel, foil, and even aluminum foil. With so many options available, the possibilities for creating unique and stunning glitter crafts are endless.

When it comes to DIY Paper Crafts for Buttons, you can easily transform plain buttons into dazzling embellishments with the help of glitter. Start by choosing the desired color and size of buttons. Apply a layer of clear adhesive over the surface of the button and then sprinkle your chosen glitter color over it. Gently tap off the excess glitter and allow it to dry completely. Your buttons will now have a beautiful glittery finish that can be used to enhance cards, scrapbook pages, or any other paper craft project.

Sequins are another versatile material that can be easily embellished with glitter. To create your own glittery sequins, apply a thin layer of adhesive over the surface of the sequin and sprinkle your desired glitter color over it. Just like with buttons, tap off the excess glitter and let it dry. Glitter sequins are perfect for adding an extra layer of texture and sparkle to any craft project.

If you want to explore the world of DIY crafts with beads, you can create unique glittery beads to use in jewelry making or other projects. Start with plain beads, either plastic or wooden, and apply a layer of clear adhesive over the surface. Before the adhesive dries, roll the bead in your chosen glitter color, making sure to coat it evenly. Let the bead dry completely before using it in your project. Glittery beads can add a touch of glamour to any jewelry piece or be used to create eye-catching decorations.

Rhinestones and gemstones are also perfect candidates for a glitter makeover. Apply clear adhesive to the surface of the stone and sprinkle glitter over it, making sure to cover the entire area. Once the adhesive has dried, you will have dazzling glittery stones that can be used to enhance accessories or other crafts.

Charms, pom-poms, feathers, and even felt can benefit from a touch of glitter. Apply adhesive to the desired area of the charm, pom-pom, or feather, and then sprinkle glitter over it. The adhesive will help the glitter to adhere to the surface, creating a glamorous and eye-catching effect. Glittery charms, pom-poms, and feathers can be used to create unique jewelry, embellishments, or even party decorations.

Cork, being a porous material, can be a bit tricky to work with when it comes to glitter. However, by applying a layer of clear adhesive to the surface of the cork and then sprinkling a generous amount of glitter over it, you can achieve a glittery effect. Just be sure to let the adhesive dry completely before handling the glittered cork.

Washi tape, fabric tape, duct tape, and masking tape offer a perfect canvas for glitter. Apply a thin layer of clear adhesive over the tape and sprinkle your chosen glitter color over it. Press the glitter firmly into the tape, making sure it adheres well. Allow the adhesive to dry completely before using the glittered tape in your crafts. Glittered tapes can be used to add a touch of sparkle to cards, scrapbook pages, or any other craft project.

Sequin waste, tinsel, and foil can also be used to create unique and interesting glitter crafts. Apply adhesive to the desired area of the material and then sprinkle glitter over it. Shake off any excess glitter and let it dry completely. You can experiment with different shapes and sizes of sequin waste, tinsel, and foil to create textured and shimmering effects in your crafts.

Lastly, even aluminum foil can be transformed into a glittery masterpiece. Apply adhesive to the surface of the foil and then sprinkle glitter over it, making sure to cover the entire area. Gently press the glitter into the adhesive and let it dry completely. Glittered aluminum foil can be used to create stunning backgrounds, embellishments, or even as a decorative element in mixed media projects.

By following the techniques and ideas presented in this chapter, you can create unique and stunning glitter crafts using a variety of materials. Whether you choose to embellish buttons, sequins, beads, rhinestones, gemstones, charms, pom-poms, feathers, felt, cork, washi tape, fabric tape, duct tape, masking tape, sequin waste, tinsel, foil, or aluminum foil, the possibilities are endless. So go ahead, embrace the glitter and let your creativity shine!.

Chapter 16: Glitter glue

- Introduction to Glitter glue

Glitter glue is a versatile and charming embellishment that adds a touch of sparkle and glam to any craft project. It is a popular choice among DIY enthusiasts due to its ease of use and ability to create eye-catching designs. In this chapter, we will explore the wonderful world of glitter glue and discuss different techniques to incorporate it into your DIY creations.

Glitter, as we all know, is a fine and shiny substance that comes in various colors and sizes. When combined with glue, it forms glitter glue, which can be easily applied to different surfaces. One of the major advantages of using glitter glue is that it eliminates the mess typically associated with loose glitter, as it provides a convenient and controlled application method.

To get started with glitter glue, you will need a few essential supplies. Firstly, make sure to have a good quality glitter glue. There are numerous brands available, so choose one that suits your preferences. You may want to consider glitter glues that are non-toxic and eco-friendly if you are working on projects involving children or if you prioritize sustainability.

In addition to glitter glue, you will also require a surface to decorate. Glitter glue can be used on various materials such as paper, fabric, wood, plastic, and metal. Depending on your project, select the appropriate surface and make sure it is clean and dry before applying the glue.

When using glitter glue, it is important to keep in mind a few key techniques. Firstly, shake the bottle well before opening to ensure that the glitter is evenly distributed within the glue. Applying the glitter glue is as simple as squeezing a small amount onto your desired surface. You can use the bottle's nozzle to apply thin lines or create intricate designs, or you can use a brush for larger areas.

Once the glitter glue is applied, allow it to dry completely. The drying time may vary depending on the brand and the thickness of the application. It is important to follow the instructions provided by the manufacturer to obtain the best results. Remember that patience is key during this step to prevent smudging or smearing the glitter glue.

Now that you have a basic understanding of glitter glue and its application technique, let's explore some ideas for incorporating it into DIY paper crafts.

Buttons, sequins, beads, rhinestones, gemstones, charms, pom-poms, feathers, felt, cork, washi tape, fabric tape, duct tape, masking tape, and sequin waste are all fantastic embellishments that can be paired with glitter glue to enhance their appearance. Imagine adding a touch of sparkle to a button flower arrangement or creating a shimmering border on a handmade card with rows of sequins.

By using glitter glue in combination with these embellishments, you can transform ordinary paper crafts into extraordinary masterpieces. Whether you decide to create your own unique designs or follow existing tutorials, the possibilities are endless when it comes to using glitter glue in DIY paper crafts.

Its convenience, controlled application, and ability to add a touch of sparkle make it a popular choice among crafters. By following the techniques mentioned above and pairing glitter glue with various embellishments, you can elevate your paper crafts to a whole new level. So, gather your supplies, unleash your creativity, and let the glitter glue work its magic!.

- Types of Glitter glue

Glitter glue is a fantastic material that not only adds a touch of sparkle to your crafts but also provides an adhesive property, making it easy to apply glitter to various surfaces.

When it comes to glitter glue, you have a plethora of options to choose from depending on your preferences and the specific look you want to achieve. One popular type is the standard glitter glue, which consists of fine glitter particles suspended in a thick glue base. This traditional version is readily available in craft stores and can be used for a wide range of projects.

If you want to add a touch of dimension and texture to your crafts, you might consider using dimensional glitter glue. This type contains larger glitter particles that create a raised effect when dry. It adds a captivating three-dimensional aspect to your artwork, making it visually interesting and unique.

For a more sophisticated and elegant touch, why not try out metallic glitter glue? As the name suggests, this type of glitter glue contains glitter particles with a metallic finish, adding a touch of glamour to your creations. The metallic shine can be especially striking when used on dark-colored surfaces, creating a stunning contrast.

If you're looking for a subtler touch of sparkle, you might find iridescent glitter glue to be a perfect option. Iridescent glitter particles have a shimmering effect that changes hues when viewed from different angles. This effect adds a magical and ethereal quality to your crafts, making them stand out in a subtle and refined manner.

For crafts that require precision application, precision tip glitter glue can be your best bet. This type of glitter glue is equipped with a specialized precision tip that allows you to apply the glue in fine lines or intricate details. It enables you to have full control over where the glitter goes, ensuring neat and precise designs in your projects.

Finally, glow-in-the-dark glitter glue is an excellent choice for projects that require an extra touch of excitement. This unique type of glitter glue contains phosphorescent pigments that absorb light and release it in the dark, creating a mesmerizing glow effect. It adds an element of surprise and fun to your crafts, especially in low-light settings.

Consider the overall theme and design of your project, and choose a glitter glue that complements it. Whether you want to create a dazzling and eye-catching masterpiece or a subtle yet enchanting composition, glitter glue offers an endless array of possibilities.

Remember to follow the manufacturer's instructions when using glitter glue, and always test it on a scrap piece of paper before applying it to your final project. With a little practice and creativity, you'll soon become adept at incorporating glitter glue into your DIY paper crafts, transforming them into sparkling works of art.

- Glitter glue Crafts Ideas

In the world of DIY crafts, glitter glue is a versatile material that can add a touch of sparkle and glamour to your creations. Whether you're making cards, scrapbooking, or engaging in any other paper crafting activity, glitter glue offers endless possibilities for creativity. So, get ready to let your artistic spirit shine!.

One idea to incorporate glitter glue into your crafts is by using it to decorate buttons. Buttons are not just functional fasteners; they can also be transformed into beautiful embellishments. With the help of glitter glue, you can elevate the ordinary button to a new level of charm and appeal. Using different colors of glitter glue, create unique designs on the surface of the buttons. You can experiment with patterns, swirls, or even write letters or words using the glitter glue. Allow the glitter glue to dry completely before using the buttons in your projects. The shimmering effect of the glitter glue will add an eye-catching element to your DIY creations.

Sequins are another fantastic material that can be enhanced with the use of glitter glue. With a wide range of colors and shapes available, sequins can make any craft project more vibrant and glamorous. To elevate the look of your sequins, try adding glitter glue to them. You can apply the glitter glue to the entire surface of the sequin or create intricate patterns and designs. This will add an extra layer of sparkle and dimension to your crafts. Once the glitter glue has dried, you can use these dazzling sequins in a variety of projects, such as cards, jewelry, or even clothing.

Beads are an essential element in jewelry making, and glitter glue can help take your beadwork to the next level. Give your beads a touch of elegance and pizzazz by applying glitter glue to them. This will create a stunning effect that will catch the light and draw attention to your designs. Experiment with different colors and combinations of glitter glue to achieve the desired look. Ensure that the glitter glue is fully dry before incorporating the beads into your jewelry pieces. The addition of glitter glue will add a glamorous and enchanting touch to your DIY jewelry creations.

Rhinestones and gemstones are popular choices for adding sparkle and glamour to crafts. By using glitter glue, you can transform these already dazzling embellishments into even more striking elements. Apply the glitter glue to the surface of the rhinestones or gemstones, allowing you to customize their appearance. You can create color combinations, gradients, or even write initials using the glitter glue. The end result will be a stunning, sparkling embellishment that will make any craft project stand out.

Charms are delightful little trinkets that can add personality and charm to your crafts. You can make them even more captivating by adding glitter glue to their surfaces. Whether you have metal charms or plastic ones, the glitter glue will adhere well to both materials. Apply the glitter glue to the charm, covering the entire surface or creating intricate designs. Allow the glitter glue to dry completely before attaching the charm to your craft project. The addition of glitter glue will make your charm even more eye-catching and enchanting.

Pom-poms are fluffy and fun embellishments that kids and adults alike enjoy using in their crafts. By incorporating glitter glue, you can take these adorable embellishments to a whole new level. Apply the glitter glue to the surface of the pom-pom, covering it completely or creating patterns. You can experiment with different colors and even mix colors to create unique effects. Once the glitter glue is dry, you can incorporate these sparkling pom-poms into a wide range of projects, from kids' crafts to home decor.

Feathers are elegant and delicate natural materials that can enhance the beauty of any craft project. With the help of glitter glue, you can make feathers even more visually captivating. Apply the glitter glue to the feathers, creating patterns or covering the entire surface. This will give the feathers a dazzling and enchanting appearance. Once the glitter glue has dried, you can use these adorned feathers in a variety of projects, such as dream catchers, decorative wreaths, or even fashion accessories.

Felt is a versatile fabric that is perfect for DIY crafts. By applying glitter glue to felt, you can create stunning designs and patterns. You can choose to cover the entire surface of the felt with glitter glue or create specific designs. This will add a dazzling touch to your felt crafts, making them more visually appealing.

Whether you're making ornaments, decorative accessories, or even clothing, the addition of glitter glue to felt will elevate your creations to new heights.

Cork is a unique material that can be used in various crafts. By incorporating glitter glue, you can transform plain cork into a dazzling element in your projects. Apply the glitter glue to the surface of the cork, covering it either fully or in specific areas. This will add a touch of sparkle and pizzazz to your crafts, making them more visually interesting. Once the glitter glue has dried, you can use the adorned cork in a variety of ways, such as making coasters, bulletin boards, or even jewelry.

Washi tape, fabric tape, duct tape, and masking tape are all fantastic materials that can add color and pattern to your crafts. By using glitter glue, you can personalize these tapes even further. Create unique designs on the surface of the tape by applying the glitter glue. You can write letters, draw patterns, or even create gradients using different colors of glitter glue. This will make your tape more visually appealing and add that charming touch to your craft projects.

Glitter glue itself is a fascinating material that can be used in numerous ways to enhance your crafts. The texture and shimmer of glitter glue can add that magical element to any project. You can use glitter glue to create patterns, write messages or names, or even mix different colors together to achieve unique effects. Experiment with different styles and techniques to find your own signature way of incorporating glitter glue into your crafts. These sparkly accents will elevate your projects and make them truly unforgettable.

The possibilities are endless, and the results will undoubtedly be dazzling and enchanting. Let your imagination run wild and have fun incorporating glitter glue into your DIY crafts.

Chapter 17: Sequin waste

- Introduction to Sequin waste

Sequin waste is an incredibly versatile and visually stunning material that can be used in various DIY projects. In this chapter, we will delve into the fascinating world of sequin waste and explore its uses in crafting.

Sequin waste is essentially the leftover trimmings from the production of sequins. These trimmings come in different shapes, sizes, and colors, making them perfect for adding sparkle and glamour to all kinds of projects. From intricate jewelry designs to eye-catching decorations, sequin waste allows you to incorporate a touch of luxury into your DIY creations.

One of the most popular uses for sequin waste is in papercraft projects. By simply gluing sequin waste onto paper, you can instantly transform a plain and ordinary piece into something dazzling and extraordinary. Whether it's a handmade card, a scrapbook page, or a wall art piece, adding sequin waste to your papercraft projects can elevate their visual appeal to a whole new level.

To get started with DIY paper crafts for sequin waste, gather the following materials:

- Sequin waste in desired colors and shapes: You can find sequin waste at most craft stores, or you can even repurpose old garments or accessories that feature sequins.

- Scrapbook paper or cardstock: Choose high-quality paper that can withstand the weight of the sequin waste.

- Craft glue: Look for a clear-drying and strong glue that can securely adhere the sequin waste to the paper.

- Scissors: You will need scissors to trim the sequin waste to the desired size and shape.

Once you have gathered these materials, follow these steps to create your DIY paper crafts with sequin waste:

1. Choose your design: Decide on the layout and composition of your project. Whether you want to create an intricate design or a simple pattern, planning ahead will help you achieve the desired result.

2. Prepare your paper: Cut the scrapbook paper or cardstock to the desired size and shape. Make sure it provides a solid foundation for the sequin waste.

3. Trim the sequin waste: Use scissors to cut the sequin waste into smaller pieces, if necessary. You can create different shapes, such as hearts, stars, or circles, to add variety to your project.

4. Apply glue: Apply a small amount of craft glue onto the backside of the sequin waste. Be mindful not to use too much glue, as it may bleed through the sequin waste and ruin the overall appearance.

5. Adhere the sequin waste: Carefully place the sequin waste onto the prepared paper, pressing it down gently to ensure it sticks securely. Repeat this step until you have achieved your desired design or pattern.

6. Let it dry: Allow the glue to dry completely before handling or displaying your finished project. This will ensure the sequin waste remains firmly attached to the paper.

With these simple steps, you can effortlessly incorporate sequin waste into your DIY paper crafts. Experiment with different colors and shapes, and let your creativity shine through. Whether you're making greeting cards, wall art, or party decorations, sequin waste will add a touch of glamour and sophistication to your creations. So go ahead, grab some sequin waste and let your imagination soar. Happy crafting!.

- Different Uses of Sequin waste

Sequin waste, a material often overlooked in the crafting world, holds immense potential when it comes to DIY projects. Whether you're a beginner or an experienced artisan, you're sure to find these ideas both inspiring and easy to implement.

One fascinating use of sequin waste is its ability to add texture and dimension to your papercraft designs. By attaching small pieces of sequin waste to your cards or scrapbooking layouts, you can create striking visual effects. Whether you prefer a subtle touch or a bold statement, the shimmer and shine of sequin waste will certainly attract attention.

Another way to utilize sequin waste in your paper crafts is by creating stunning backgrounds. You can layer sequin waste over colored paper or cardstock, securing it in place with craft glue or double-sided adhesive. This technique adds depth and interest to your designs, making them stand out in a sea of ordinary projects.

Sequin waste can also be transformed into unique embellishments for your paper crafts. By cutting the sequin waste into various shapes and sizes, you can create custom buttons, flowers, or other decorative elements. These embellishments not only add visual interest but also provide tactile stimulation, enriching the overall sensory experience of your crafts.

For those who enjoy mixed media projects, sequin waste can be combined with other materials such as beads, rhinestones, and gemstones to create stunning works of art. From jewelry to home décor items, the possibilities are endless. By allowing your creativity to roam free, you can turn humble sequin waste into something truly extraordinary.

Furthermore, sequin waste can be combined with charms, pom-poms, feathers, and other materials to create whimsical and playful paper crafts. Whether you're making greeting cards, gift tags, or party decorations, these unique elements are sure to delight the recipient and make your creations truly one-of-a-kind.

Sequin waste can also be incorporated into mixed media collages by layering it with other materials such as felt, cork, and fabric tape. This creates an intriguing contrast of textures and adds a touch of glamour to your artwork. The versatility of sequin waste allows you to experiment with various combinations and achieve stunning results.

To enhance the dazzling effect of sequin waste, you can pair it with glitter, glitter glue, or tinsel. These sparkling accents will make your crafts shine and add a touch of festive flair. Additionally, incorporating foil or aluminum foil into your sequin waste designs can create a metallic sheen that elevates the overall aesthetic of your paper crafts.

Its ability to add texture, dimension, and visual interest to your projects is truly remarkable. By employing various techniques and combining sequin waste with other materials, you can create a wide range of eye-catching and unique designs. So grab your sequin waste and embark on a creative journey that will leave you with breathtaking paper crafts that are bound to impress.

- Sequin waste Crafts Ideas

Sequin waste, often referred to as sequin trim or trimmings, is a versatile crafting material that adds sparkle and glamour to any project. In this guide, I will provide you with a detailed analysis of DIY Paper Crafts for Buttons, Sequins, Beads, Rhinestones, Gemstones, Charms, Pom-poms, Feathers, Felt, Cork, Washi tape, Fabric tape, Duct tape, Masking tape, Glitter, Glitter glue, Sequin waste, Tinsel, Foil, and Aluminum foil. Let's dive in!.

Sequin waste can be used in a myriad of ways to create stunning paper crafts. One popular idea is to use it to embellish handmade greeting cards. To achieve this, simply cut a piece of cardstock to your desired size and fold it in half to create a card. Now, take some sequin waste and adhere it to the front of the card using a glue stick or double-sided tape. You can arrange the sequins in a pattern or create a random design for a whimsical touch. Finish it off by adding a button, bead, or gemstone in the center of some of the sequins for an extra pop of color and dimension.

Another creative use of sequin waste is to make paper ornaments. Start by cutting out a shape from sturdy cardstock, such as a star, heart, or Christmas tree. Punch a hole at the top for hanging. Next, apply glue to the entire surface of the shape and carefully press the sequin waste onto it. You can experiment with different colors and sizes of sequins to create a dazzling effect. Sprinkle some glitter over the wet glue for added sparkle. Once the glue is dry, thread a piece of string or ribbon through the hole and tie it in a loop to hang your ornament.

If you're looking for a more interactive paper craft, how about creating a sequined spinner? Start by cutting a circle out of cardstock and divide it into sections using a ruler and pencil. Apply glue to one section at a time and cover it with sequin waste. Repeat this process for each section until the entire circle is covered. Attach a button or bead to the center of the circle with a brad. Now, attach a string or ribbon to the brad, leaving enough length for the spinner to hang freely. Give it a spin and watch the sequins shimmer and shine!.

Whether you're making greeting cards, ornaments, or spinners, the possibilities are endless. Get creative and experiment with different colors, sizes, and patterns to create unique and eye-catching designs. With a little bit of imagination and some sequin waste, you'll be able to create stunning paper crafts that are sure to impress.

Chapter 18: Tinsel

- Introduction to Tinsel

Tinsel crafts are a fantastic way to add sparkle and glamour to your DIY projects. Whether you're embellishing cards, ornaments, or home decor items, tinsel is a versatile material that can truly elevate your creations. In this chapter, we will explore various ways to incorporate tinsel into your crafts, providing you with inspiration and step-by-step instructions to get you started.

Tinsel is a thin, shiny material that is primarily made from metallic strands. It is traditionally used as Christmas tree decoration, but its unique texture and shine make it a valuable asset in various DIY projects. Tinsel comes in a range of colors, sizes, and finishes, enabling you to find the perfect match for your creative vision.

To begin working with tinsel, you'll need a few essential supplies. Firstly, gather some adhesive options such as glue or adhesive tapes. These will be needed to secure the tinsel to your craft projects. Next, make sure to have a pair of scissors, as you may need to trim and cut the tinsel to the desired length or shape. Finally, have a clear workspace and organize your tinsel colors and styles, ensuring they are easily accessible.

When working with tinsel, you have several options for applying it to your crafts. Here are a few techniques you can explore:

1. Wrapping: A simple and effective technique is to wrap tinsel around objects like gift boxes, wreaths, or frames. Start by applying a thin layer of glue or using double-sided adhesive tape to the object. Place the end of the tinsel on the glue or tape and gently wrap it around, securing it as you go. Continue wrapping until the desired coverage is achieved, and then cut off any excess tinsel.

2. Creating Tinsel Accents: If you wish to add smaller tinsel details to your crafts, cut small sections of tinsel and adhere them to your project with glue or small adhesive dots. These accents can be used to highlight specific areas or create a sparkling border.

3. Tinsel Pompoms: Combine the whimsy of pompoms with the sparkle of tinsel by creating tinsel pompoms. Cut a long strip of tinsel and fold it lengthwise multiple times, creating a layered bundle. Secure the center of the bundle tightly with a small piece of craft wire or string. Then, using scissors, start cutting the looped ends of the tinsel to create the signature pompom shape. Fluff and shape the tinsel until you achieve the desired pompom look. These tinsel pompoms can be used as decorative accents or attached to various crafts such as bookmarks or keychains.

4. Tinsel Embellishments: Experiment with different techniques to create unique tinsel embellishments. For instance, you can cut small sections of tinsel and arrange them into shapes like stars, hearts, or snowflakes. Secure these shapes with glue, and once dry, they can be used as standalone embellishments or affixed to other crafts.

Remember, the key to successfully working with tinsel is to experiment and let your creativity flourish. Embrace the shiny and festive nature of tinsel, and don't be afraid to try new techniques and combinations.

With its versatility and ability to add glitz and glamour to crafts, tinsel opens up a world of possibilities. From wrapping and creating accents to making tinsel pompoms and embellishments, there are endless ways to make your crafts shine with the magic of tinsel. So, grab your supplies, get creative, and let the tinsel sparkles mesmerize your DIY creations!.

- Different Uses of Tinsel

Tinsel is an incredibly versatile material that can add a touch of sparkle and glamour to any DIY project. In this chapter, we will explore different creative uses of tinsel and how you can incorporate it into various crafts. Tinsel is a thin, shiny thread-like material made from metallic or reflective materials such as aluminum foil or plastic. Its unique properties make it perfect for adding a festive and eye-catching element to your projects. Here are some ideas on how to use tinsel in your DIY creations.

One way to use tinsel is in DIY paper crafts. You can add tinsel to buttons, sequins, beads, rhinestones, gemstones, charms, pom-poms, feathers, felt, cork, washi tape, fabric tape, duct tape, masking tape, glitter, glitter glue, sequin waste, and foil. By attaching pieces of tinsel to these crafting materials, you can instantly elevate their appearance and make them look more luxurious and glamorous. For example, you can glue tinsel to the edges of paper buttons or incorporate it into the design of sequined motifs. The possibilities are endless!.

Tinsel is also great for creating stunning holiday decorations. You can wrap tinsel around a wreath frame, creating a sparkling base for your seasonal embellishments. Alternatively, you can weave tinsel strands through an embroidery hoop to create a festive hoop art. Tinsel can also be used to create beautiful ornaments for your Christmas tree. Simply shape the tinsel into desired shapes such as stars, hearts, or snowflakes, and attach them to a foam or cardstock backing.

In addition to paper crafts and holiday decorations, tinsel can be incorporated into fashion accessories and jewelry. You can use tinsel to make statement necklaces, earrings, bracelets, or even belt buckles. By pairing tinsel with beads, gemstones, or rhinestones, you can create unique and eye-catching designs. Tinsel can also be used to embellish hair accessories such as headbands, hairpins, or barrettes, adding a touch of festive flair to any hairstyle.

Furthermore, tinsel can be used in home decor projects to create a whimsical and vibrant atmosphere. You can wrap tinsel around picture frames, mirrors, or vases to instantly transform them into glamorous pieces. Tinsel can also be used to create stunning table centerpieces by arranging it around candles or floral arrangements. By combining tinsel with other materials such as fabric, ribbon, or twine, you can create stunning garlands, banners, or even wall art.

When working with tinsel, it is important to handle it with care as it can be delicate and easily tangled. Use a small amount of clear adhesive to secure the tinsel to your crafting material, ensuring it stays in place. Additionally, you can trim the tinsel to desired lengths or shapes using a pair of sharp scissors. Experiment with different colors, textures, and thicknesses of tinsel to achieve various effects and make your projects uniquely yours.

Whether you are creating paper crafts, holiday decorations, fashion accessories, or home decor items, tinsel can add a touch of sparkle and glamour that takes your creations to the next level. So, grab some tinsel and let your creativity shine!.

- Tinsel Crafts Ideas

In this chapter, we will explore the exciting world of tinsel crafts and how you can incorporate this sparkling material into your DIY projects. Tinsel adds a touch of glamour and shine to any craft, making it a versatile material that can be used in various creative ways. So, let's dive into the art of tinsel crafting!.

Tinsel can be used in a wide range of DIY crafts, including cards, ornaments, home decor, and jewelry. Its shiny and reflective nature instantly catches the eye and adds an element of festivity and celebration to any project. Whether you're looking to create a glittering holiday ornament or an eye-catching piece of jewelry, tinsel can be a perfect choice.

One popular tinsel craft idea is to create tinsel wreaths. These wreaths are not only beautiful but also fun to make. Start by purchasing a foam wreath form from your local craft store. Wrap the wreath form with tinsel, securing it with hot glue as you go along. Once the wreath is completely covered in tinsel, you can add decorative ornaments, ribbons, or even small LED lights to give it a festive touch.

Another way to use tinsel in your crafts is by incorporating it into your holiday cards. Cut out various shapes from cardstock, such as Christmas trees, snowflakes, or even animals, and then embellish them with tinsel. Simply apply a thin layer of glue to the desired areas, and then sprinkle tinsel over it. Let it dry, and your cards will have a beautiful and dimensional look.

If you're a jewelry enthusiast, you can experiment with tinsel to create stunning statement pieces. For example, you can make tinsel earrings by creating shapes out of wire and then wrapping tinsel around them. Add earring hooks, and you'll have a unique and eye-catching accessory to wear. Tinsel can also be used to embellish necklaces, bracelets, and even hair accessories.

To add a touch of glamour to your home decor, consider creating tinsel garlands. These garlands can be made by stringing tinsel through a thin ribbon or twine. You can use different colors of tinsel to create a festive theme, or stick to a single color for an elegant and sophisticated look. Hang these garlands on your Christmas tree, mantelpiece, or even along your staircase to instantly transform your space.

Apart from these specific craft ideas, tinsel can also be used in various other ways. For example, you can use it to wrap gifts, decorate Christmas stockings, or even create tinsel pom-poms for a fun and whimsical touch. The possibilities are truly endless when it comes to tinsel crafts.

Its shiny and reflective nature instantly adds a touch of glamour and festivity to any craft. Whether you choose to create wreaths, cards, jewelry, or home decor, tinsel is sure to make your creations sparkle and shine. So, grab some tinsel and let your creativity shine through!.

Chapter 19: Foil

- Introduction to Foil

In the world of DIY crafts, foil is a versatile and captivating material that can add an element of shine and sophistication to your projects. Whether you are a beginner or an experienced artisan, learning how to incorporate foil into your creations will open up a plethora of creative possibilities. In this chapter, we will explore the wonderful world of foil and provide you with step-by-step instructions on how to incorporate foil into your DIY paper crafts.

To start with, let's discuss the requirements for working with foil. The primary material we will focus on is aluminum foil, a thin and pliable sheet that is readily available and easy to manipulate. Other types of foil, such as gold or silver foil, can also be used, but we will mainly focus on aluminum foil due to its affordability and accessibility. You will also need a few basic crafting supplies, including scissors, glue or adhesive, a ruler, and a bone folder or a similar tool for smoothing out wrinkles and creases.

Now that we have covered the necessary materials, let's delve into the process of incorporating foil into your DIY paper crafts. One of the most popular methods to transfer foil onto paper is using heat. You can achieve this by utilizing a heat-activated adhesive or a laminating machine. The process involves applying heat to the foil, which activates the adhesive and allows it to bond with the paper.

To start, create your desired design on the paper using buttons, sequins, beads, rhinestones, gemstones, charms, pom-poms, feathers, felt, cork, Washi tape, fabric tape, duct tape, masking tape, glitter, glitter glue, sequin waste, tinsel, or any other embellishments you choose. Arrange them in a pleasing pattern and secure them in place with glue or adhesive.

Next, cut a piece of aluminum foil slightly larger than the area you wish to cover with foil. Place it over your design, ensuring that the shiny side of the foil is facing up. Smooth out any wrinkles or bubbles with a bone folder or a similar tool, being careful not to damage the surface of your project.

Once the foil is in place, you can activate the adhesive by using a heat source. If you are using a heat-activated adhesive, carefully apply heat to the foil using a heat tool or an iron set on a low temperature. Be cautious not to apply too much heat, as it can melt the foil or cause it to wrinkle.

If you are using a laminating machine, follow the manufacturer's instructions to feed your project through the machine. The heat generated by the machine will activate the adhesive and bond the foil to the paper.

Once the adhesive has been activated, allow your project to cool down before handling it. Once cooled, gently peel off the foil to reveal your dazzling design. You can further enhance the look by adding additional embellishments or details, such as outlines or accents with markers or pens.

By following the steps outlined above and experimenting with different materials and techniques, you can create stunning designs that are bound to impress. So, unleash your creativity and let foil become your secret weapon in the world of DIY embellishments!.

- Types of Foil

In the enchanting world of DIY crafts, the use of foil brings a touch of shimmer and flair to any project. From paper crafts to embellishments, foil is a versatile material that can add a luxurious and eye-catching effect.

When it comes to foil, one of the most commonly used varieties is aluminum foil. This type of foil is highly pliable and can be easily manipulated to create interesting shapes and designs. It's ideal for adding a metallic sheen to your crafts and can be used as a base layer or as an accent. Whether you're crafting cards, scrapbooking, or making decorative elements, aluminum foil opens up a world of possibilities.

Another type of foil that is worthy of attention is sequin waste. This innovative material is made by binding discarded sequins to a flexible backing, creating a sheet of sequins in various shapes and sizes. Sequin waste can be used to add a dazzling touch to your DIY projects, be it for jewelry, clothing, or home decor. Its lightweight nature makes it easy to work with and allows for endless creativity.

Moving on, we come to tinsel foil. This type of foil features thin, glossy, and metallic strips that are perfect for adding a touch of sparkle to your crafts. Tinsel foil is commonly used during festive seasons or for adding a celebratory vibe to your creations. You can use this foil to create borders, accents, or even as a background for your artwork. Let your imagination run wild and transform your projects with this dazzling material.

Foil comes in a wide array of colors and finishes, each bringing its unique charm to your crafts. Whether you're after a classic metallic shine, a vibrant pop of color, or even a holographic effect, there's a foil to suit every creative vision. Experiment with floral, animal, or abstract prints to add an extra layer of visual interest to your projects.

As you venture into the world of embellishments, you'll discover that foil is a go-to material for adding dimension and sophistication to your creations. Whether you're working with gemstones, charms, or rhinestones, foil can be used as a backdrop to highlight and enhance these elements. The reflective properties of foil will make your embellishments truly shine and take center stage.

When it comes to using foil in your DIY crafts, ensure that you have the necessary tools at hand. A good pair of scissors is essential for cutting and shaping the foil, while adhesive sprays or glue dots will ensure a secure and long-lasting bond. Additionally, consider investing in heat transfer foils, which can be applied using a heat source such as an iron or a laminator. This technique allows for a more professional and seamless finish.

Its versatility, sparkle, and ability to elevate your crafts make it an invaluable asset to your creative endeavors. From the shimmering elegance of aluminum foil to the playful glimmer of tinsel foil, there are endless possibilities to explore. So go forth, let your creativity soar, and see how foil can transform your DIY projects into works of art.

- Foil Crafts Ideas

Foil is a versatile material that adds shine and elegance to any DIY project. In this guide, I will provide detailed instructions on creating various DIY foil crafts.

First, let's explore the materials and tools you will need for these foil crafts. Besides foil, you will require a few essential items like scissors, glue, and a crafting board or surface. Depending on the specific project, you may also need additional tools such as a cutting machine, embossing tools, or punches. Gather these materials and tools before getting started.

One idea is to create DIY foil paper crafts using buttons. Begin by cutting a piece of foil slightly larger than the button you wish to cover. Place the button in the middle of the foil and fold the foil edges tightly around it, securing it in place. This technique not only covers the button with a beautiful metallic sheen but also adds a touch of sophistication to your projects.

Another fascinating idea is to incorporate foil into your DIY projects with sequins. Start by cutting a piece of foil in the desired shape and size. Apply glue directly onto the sequin and carefully press it onto the foil, ensuring it adheres firmly. You can experiment with different shapes, colors, and patterns to create eye-catching foil sequin designs that will shine and sparkle.

Beads can also be enhanced with foil to create unique and stunning DIY crafts. Begin by threading your chosen beads onto a wire or string, leaving enough length on both ends to tie a knot. Cut a strip of foil, long enough to cover the bead, and wrap it around the bead, securing it with glue or overlapping the edges neatly. The foil will lend a glossy and luxurious appearance to your beadwork, making it stand out in jewelry, accessories, or even home decor items.

If you want to add a touch of glamour to your projects, consider using foil in combination with rhinestones or gemstones. Place a small amount of glue onto the stone's base and carefully position it onto the foil, applying gentle pressure to ensure it adheres securely. This technique will elevate your crafts, turning them into eye-catching pieces that exude elegance and charm.

Charms, pom-poms, feathers, felt, cork, washi tape, fabric tape, duct tape, masking tape, glitter, glitter glue, sequin waste, tinsel, and aluminum foil are other materials that can be combined with foil to create stunning and original designs. The possibilities for incorporating foil into various DIY crafts are endless, so let your creativity flow and experiment with different combinations to achieve your desired results.

Remember to always follow the specific instructions for each DIY project you undertake, and take your time to ensure precision and attention to detail.

" With this knowledge and your artistic skills, you can now begin creating beautiful and unique foil craft projects that will impress and inspire others. Enjoy the process and happy crafting!.

Chapter 20: Aluminum foil

- Introduction to Aluminum foil

Aluminum foil is an incredibly versatile material that can be used in a variety of DIY projects. Its flexibility, durability, and reflective properties make it ideal for crafting purposes. In this chapter, we will delve into the world of aluminum foil and explore the various ways in which it can be incorporated into your DIY endeavors.

When it comes to DIY paper crafts, aluminum foil can add a touch of uniqueness and sophistication to your creations. Its metallic sheen stands out and catches the light, creating eye-catching effects. Whether you're working with buttons, sequins, beads, rhinestones, gemstones, charms, pom-poms, feathers, felt, cork, washi tape, fabric tape, duct tape, masking tape, glitter, glitter glue, sequin waste, tinsel, or foil itself, aluminum foil can elevate the overall aesthetic of your projects.

One of the simplest ways to use aluminum foil in DIY paper crafts is by creating embellishments. Cut out various shapes and sizes from the foil, such as stars, flowers, or geometrical patterns, and adhere them onto your crafts using glue. The reflective surface of the foil will not only add dimension but also provide an interesting contrast against the background materials.

Another popular technique for incorporating aluminum foil into your projects is embossing. Embossing involves creating raised designs on paper by applying pressure and heat to the foil. To emboss with aluminum foil, you will need an embossing machine or handheld tools. Simply place the foil between the embossing folder and run it through the machine or apply pressure with the tool. The result is a beautifully textured, metallic design that adds depth and elegance to your creations.

For those looking to add a touch of shimmer and shine, aluminum foil can be used as a backing for transparent or translucent materials such as sequins or gemstones. By adhering these elements onto the foil, you create a reflective surface that enhances their sparkle and enhances the overall visual impact.

Additionally, aluminum foil can be used to create unique textures on paper. By crinkling, folding, or scrunching the foil and layering it onto your crafts, you can achieve interesting patterns and designs. Experiment with different folding techniques and combine them with other materials to create visually captivating effects.

Moreover, aluminum foil can be painted, colored, or further embellished to suit your desired aesthetic. Whether you prefer a rustic, aged look or a vibrant, metallic finish, aluminum foil can be easily customized to suit your creative vision. Use paints, markers, or inks to add colors or blend different shades for a more intricate look.

It's worth noting that while aluminum foil is a versatile material, it does have its limitations. It may not be suitable for projects that require heavy-duty or long-lasting durability, as it can tear or crumple over time. However, for decorative and temporary purposes, aluminum foil is an excellent choice that can add a touch of uniqueness and sophistication to your DIY projects.

From creating embellishments and adding texture to embossing and creating eye-catching backings, aluminum foil offers endless possibilities. With a little creativity and experimentation, you can incorporate aluminum foil into your crafting repertoire and elevate your projects to a whole new level. So go ahead and explore the fascinating world of aluminum foil and unleash your creativity!.

It emphasizes the versatility and potential applications of aluminum foil in crafting, showcasing its ability to enhance visual appeal and add uniqueness to various materials and techniques.

- Different Uses of Aluminum foil

Aluminum foil is a versatile material that can be found in any household. While its primary use is for wrapping food, there are actually numerous creative ways to incorporate aluminum foil into your DIY projects. .

Buttons can be transformed into unique pieces by using aluminum foil. Simply cut out small pieces of foil and fold them around the buttons, giving them a metallic appearance. You can then use these foil-covered buttons as embellishments for clothing, accessories, or even as decorative accents for paper crafts. The foil adds a touch of shine and dimension to your projects.

Sequins can also benefit from aluminum foil. By sticking them onto foil and cutting around the edges, you create individual sequin shapes that you can then attach onto various surfaces. These foil-backed sequins can be used to create stunning designs on cards, scrapbook layouts, or any other paper crafts. The foil backing enhances the sparkle and reflection of the sequins, making them stand out even more.

Beads, rhinestones, and gemstones can all be accented with aluminum foil to create unique and eye-catching jewelry pieces. Simply wrap small pieces of foil around the base of the beads or stones and secure them in place with adhesive. This technique adds a metallic shine to your jewelry designs and gives them a more modern and edgy look.

When working with charms, pom-poms, feathers, felt, and cork, aluminum foil can be used to create interesting textures and effects. By wrapping these materials with foil, you can achieve a metallic finish that adds a touch of sophistication to your projects. This technique works particularly well for decorative accents on home décor items, such as picture frames or ornaments.

Washi tape, fabric tape, duct tape, and masking tape can all be combined with aluminum foil to create unique and custom designs. Simply apply strips of tape onto aluminum foil, and then use scissors or craft punches to cut out shapes or patterns. These foil-backed tape designs can be used to decorate various surfaces, such as notebooks, gift boxes, or even furniture. The metallic shine of the foil adds a luxurious touch to your tape designs.

Glitter and glitter glue can also be enhanced with aluminum foil. By sprinkling foil flakes onto wet glue or mixing foil shreds into glitter glue, you can create a dazzling effect that catches the light and adds extra sparkle to your projects. This technique works particularly well for card making, scrapbooking, or any other projects that require a touch of glam.

Sequin waste, tinsel, and foil itself can also be incorporated into your crafting projects. Sequin waste, also known as punchinella or sequin mesh, can be covered with foil to create unique stencils or masks for spray inks or texture pastes. Tinsel can be wrapped with foil to create shimmering garlands or embellishments for holiday-themed crafts. And for foil itself, you can experiment with various techniques, such as embossing or die-cutting, to create intricate designs that easily add a metallic touch to any project.

From adding shine and dimension to buttons, sequins, beads, and gemstones, to creating interesting textures with charms, pom-poms, feathers, and felt, aluminum foil is a valuable tool for crafting. Whether you are decorating with washi tape, fabric tape, duct tape, or masking tape, or adding sparkle to your projects with glitter, glitter glue, sequin waste, or tinsel, aluminum foil can elevate your creations and make them truly unique. So next time you reach for that roll of aluminum foil, think beyond the kitchen and explore its potential in your crafting endeavors.

- Aluminum foil Crafts Ideas

In this chapter, we will explore the many possibilities of creating DIY crafts using aluminum foil. Aluminum foil is a versatile material that can be easily manipulated, making it perfect for a wide range of craft projects. Whether you are new to crafting or a seasoned artisan, these ideas are sure to inspire your creativity and help you create beautiful and unique pieces.

Before we dive into the different aluminum foil craft ideas, let's talk about the materials you will need for these projects. Of course, the main material is aluminum foil, but depending on the specific project, you may also need other materials such as glue, scissors, paint, and various embellishments like buttons, sequins, beads, and more. It is always a good idea to gather all the necessary materials before you begin your craft project, as it will ensure a smooth and enjoyable crafting experience.

One popular craft idea using aluminum foil is creating embossed designs. To achieve this effect, you will need a piece of cardboard or foam board as your base. Cut the aluminum foil slightly larger than the base and place it on top, making sure it is smooth and free of any wrinkles. Next, use a dull pencil or a stylus to trace your desired design onto the foil, pressing firmly but not too hard. The pressure of the pencil will create an embossed effect on the foil, giving your design a three-dimensional look. You can experiment with different designs and patterns to create unique and stunning pieces.

Another aluminum foil craft idea is creating jewelry. You can make beautiful and eye-catching earrings, necklaces, and bracelets using aluminum foil. Begin by cutting out the desired shape using scissors or a craft punch. Then, embellish the foil shape with sequins, rhinestones, gemstones, or beads of your choice. You can glue these embellishments onto the foil using craft glue or a hot glue gun. Allow the glue to dry completely before attaching any findings such as jump rings, earring hooks, or chain links. With just a few materials and some creativity, you can have a stunning piece of jewelry that is unique to your style.

Aluminum foil can also be used to create decorative elements for home decor. For example, you can make stunning wall art by cutting out various shapes or words from the foil and adhering them to a canvas or a wooden plaque. You can paint the foil before attaching it to add a pop of color or create a metallic effect. Experiment with different techniques such as crumpling the foil or painting it with different colors to achieve different textures and finishes.

In addition to these ideas, you can also use aluminum foil to create gift wrap and gift tags, decorative flowers, holiday ornaments, and so much more. The possibilities are truly endless when it comes to crafting with aluminum foil.

Remember, the key to successful aluminum foil crafts is to experiment and let your creativity flow. Don't be afraid to try new techniques or combine different materials to create unique and personalized pieces. So grab your materials and let your imagination soar as you embark on your aluminum foil crafting journey!.